THE ART OF
Joyful
LIVING

THE ART OF
Joyful
LIVING

SWAMI RAMA

The Himalayan International Institute
of Yoga Science and Philosophy
of the U.S.A.
Honesdale, Pennsylvania

© 1989, © 1996 by Himalayan International Institute of
Yoga Science and Philosophy of the U.S.A.
RR 1 Box 1129
Honesdale, Pennsylvania 18431-9706

03 02 01   8 7 6
Sixth Printing, 2001

Library of Congress Cataloging-in-Oublication Data

Rama, Swami, 1925-1996
    The art of joyful living: meditation and daily life /
by Swami Rama
      p.   cm.
    ISBN 0-89389-117-7
    1. meditation. 2. Spiritual life. 3. Conduct of life.
I. Title.   89-29348
BL627.R336 1989   CIP
291.4'3—dc20

Contents

Foreword

In this beautiful book, Swami Rama teaches us that we are all residents of two worlds: the external world of relationships, work, family, and community, and the internal world of our deepest inner reality. The greatest of all human achievements is to live skillfully in both of these worlds and learn to balance these two aspects of life.

We spend most of our lives learning the skills necessary to survive and function well in the external world—to communicate and relate well with others, to work, and to manage our own behavior. We receive very little instruction, however, in the techniques for knowing the internal world, and so our lives are often unbalanced and lack a sense of direction and purpose.

Recognizing the importance of this internal world leads the thoughtful and sensitive individual to a desire to know himself or herself on all levels, and to achieve this goal, the technique of meditation has been taught throughout the world, in diverse cultures.

According to the lessons Swami Rama shares with us, our understanding of how to prepare ourselves for meditation is actually more important than the amount of time we devote to sitting for meditation itself. At first, we deal with the question of preparing the body so that we can sit comfortably in meditation, and we soon begin to notice the impact that stretching exercises, aerobic exercise, relaxation, and pranayama all have on the quietness and stillness of the body. We also become increasingly aware of how our skill in managing and balancing the issues of food, sex, and sleep helps us to deepen our experience.

We next begin to notice a second level of preparation needed to sit quietly in meditation: the level of managing our minds, emotions, personalities, and relationships so that these do not disturb or interfere with our ability to be still and inwardly focused. It is our moods, conflicts, negative emotions, and mental restlessness that really provide the disturbances to our meditation. Conflicts or disturbance on the level of mind and emotions are also often the seed of difficulties in managing some of the "physical" issues—such as balancing food intake or sleep, and thus exert another indirect effect on our experience of quietness in meditation.

At some point, we may recognize that finding ways of quieting the "noise" generated by our minds and personalities becomes the most important phase of our preparation for meditation. As we manage our work and relationships, and understand our mental processes more fully, there seem to be successively fewer distractions in our meditation. Resolving the issues of external life fosters increasing quiet as we sit to meditate, which then, in turn, contributes to increasing clarity, energy, and self-confidence in handling other external involvements.

The specific techniques of meditation have been taught systematically by Swami Rama in his books, *Lectures on Yoga, Enlightenment Without God,* and *Path of Fire and Light.* Similarly, the process of preparing the body for meditation, by utilizing hatha yoga, relaxation, pranayama techniques, and an awareness of the subtleties of diet and nutrition, have been discussed extensively in other Institute publications. The purpose of this book, however, is to help sincere and motivated students of meditation to understand some of the other ways they can prepare themselves for exploring the Inner Reality.

From the perspective of this tradition, our goal is to develop ourselves on all levels, and at the same time, to become more loving, dynamic, and creative in our involvements with the external world. As Swamiji has been demonstrating for many years, the path of meditation and spirituality is not a withdrawal from the world based on frustration or fear, but a skillful process of learning to be in the world and yet not of the world. Our success in dealing with the external world is both the beneficiary of, and the test of, our meditative development.

The various chapters of this book were originally separate lectures given by Swamiji in 1989, which led to many requests that this information be presented in written form. The lectures were transcribed and edited, and supplemented by new material written by Swamiji. To preserve the clarity and flow of each chapter, some re-emphasis of concepts and ideas exists. We are happy to make these teachings available to Swamiji's students around the world and certain that they will be of great benefit.

Kay Gendron, Ph.D.
Himalayan Institute

Chapter 1

Knowing Your Own True Self

You all want to know that reality or truth which is eternal; you want to experience that state of peace and equilibrium that is your essential nature. And yet the mind and personality prevent you from experiencing that finest level of yourself—the Center of Consciousness within. In the ancient teachings it is said that time, space, and causation are the three prime conditionings or filters that affect the mind; however, you can lead your mind beyond these conditions.

Time is the most powerful of all the "filters" that condition the mind. It is a powerful filter of reality. For example, perhaps you are very sad today, but even then, a time comes during the day when you laugh. Or perhaps today you have been laughing and feeling good; still a time will come when you become sad. Thus, time affects your mind. Every state of mind is transitory and limited by time.

It is important to understand and recognize how time affects the mind. You can better understand the effect of time by considering the nature of space. If you can fully understand how space is created, then time will no longer deter you; you will go beyond both time and space. For example, if I draw two lines, then there is space between the first line and another. If there is no space, there is only One; then where is time? Time and space exist only when there is division, when you are divided within yourself. When you are One with yourself, the Self of all, then time, space, and causation—the three conditionings and limitations of the mind—are left behind and you go forward to a higher experience.

The human endeavor and purpose is not actually to attain God. Since childhood you have all been listening in church and to your parents, who have told you that you should want God, but in fact, you already have Him, because He is omnipresent. What you don't have, what you have not attained, is yourself. So your endeavor should really be to attain yourself. When you truly know yourself, when you realize yourself, then you will understand that you have also realized God. That which you call God today, you will understand fully when you know yourself on the deepest level.

I am not talking about knowing the "mere self" alone. There are actually two concepts of "self": the first is the mere self and the second is the real Self. The mere self is that self which changes over time, which has been conditioned, learned, and acquired. Nature changes, forms change, and even your name changes, but the real Self never changes.

If the real Self changed, then the very *summum bonum* of life would be changed, and then life itself would crumble. Everything that exists—all that can be seen, all that moves and changes, this whole wheel of the universe—rotates on the foundation of that which does not move. If that unmoving something starts to move, then this external wheel of the universe will no longer rotate. The external frame of a wheel moves, yet the center hub of the wheel remains steady. If the hub moves, then the whole wheel will not rotate. In that same manner, there is something in you that moves; you are like a wheel in motion. But there is also something in you, a hub within you, that does not move, yet it moves with you wherever you go. You should try to understand this metaphor.

I am talking about that Self which is the very cause of all your movements. Consider this a little more subtly: a wheel moves because of its spokes. Your hub is within and the external wheel is outside, and yet if there are no spokes the wheel will not move. You are not moving in the world because of your soul, the hub; you are moving because of the various faculties of mind, which are the spokes—you cannot ignore their influence. Reality is your center hub, but to know that inner cause of all your movements, you first have to know the nature of these faculties which make you move.

There are three aspects of yourself to understand: that which moves, that through which it moves, and that which is the cause of the movement. You have to clearly understand these three aspects to fully understand yourself. The nature of the hub within cannot be imagined with the mind, because your mind is conditioned by time, space, and causation. Your human effort is to know your entire Self—the self that moves, the subtler self that motivates us to move, and the subtler Self that is the cause of movement. That is why you should distinguish between the mere self and the real Self.

We will explore the mere self first. Perhaps your mother gave you a particular name and told you that you were far superior to other children. Then, you took that idea into your mind, although you never tried to understand it, and now you act according to that idea of your superiority. That is your mere self, the sense of self you acquired. When you are involved in that mere self so deeply, you are strengthening and feeding your ego again and again, and because of that, your development does not go beyond that ego or limited sense of self.

That which separates you from your real Self—the

whole and real—is your ego. You may wonder how you can cut down that ego or may try to tear it down or forget it, but that's not possible. Instead, you have to learn to "polish" or train your ego. When the ego becomes aware of the Reality, it is trained, and then the ego is useful. If the ego does not remain aware of the Reality, then the ego becomes unhelpful; it is then harmful or an obstacle.

The mind is a great tool that you can learn to use when you know about the various faculties of the mind. The mind has four main faculties, which we will describe briefly here and more fully in a later chapter. The first is ego, or *ahamkara,* which is one of the most prominent and powerful. That which says, "this is mine, this is me," is ego. When you become dishonest you become egotistical, and whenever you are egotistical, you are also dishonest. The more egotistical you are, the more dishonest you are with yourself, and then your dishonesty is also reflected to others.

Just as the ego is powerful, so also is *buddhi,* the faculty of intellect very powerful. Buddhi is the particular faculty of mind that has three main functions: it knows, decides, and judges.

Manas is the faculty which produces data for you from the external world. It is also the function which doubts and questions. The final function is *chitta,* the reservoir of impressions and memories. Learning how to coordinate these four functions of mind is very important and will be discussed in a later chapter. For now, it is important to understand that they are not the Self.

If you want to know your true Self, you should understand that it is neither your mind nor your personality. The personality is something outside your Self. The word "personality" comes from its root word, *persona,* a Greek word that refers to coverings and masks. If you remove all the coverings and veils of your personality, one by one, you will find the real Light within. You will find the real Self. In meditation you don't eliminate any aspect of yourself or your ego, but you learn to go inside to this Source and this Light. You are not searching for something outside yourself that is difficult to find. You are searching for someone who is already within you, so it is actually easy to find. But unfortunately, the training to do that is usually not present. Since your childhood you have not been trained to see things in the internal world; instead, you have been taught to see things and to watch and judge things in the external world. No one teaches you how to look within, to find something within, and to go to the Source within. This subtle teaching is missing in your home life.

In other times something unique and interesting took place: in the family's education, the mother-in-law had a great responsibility. As soon as her daughter-in-law came to the home, the mother-in-law would take her outside and say, "Do you see that star?" And the daughter-in-law would reply, "Oh, yes, everyone sees that."

And the mother-in-law would continue, "Do you see the star next to it?" And for a moment the daughter would be quiet, and then she would reply, "Now I can see it."

And the mother would continue, "Yes, it is also possible to see that, but do you see still another star next to that?" And the daughter would answer, "No." The mother-in-law would then say, "My duty is to help you to see that." My duty as a teacher is to show you how to see that which is more subtle, that which is not easily seen, to understand not only the external wheel and these various functions of mind, but to see and know the Source within. The day that you see that face to face, you have accomplished your work as a human being—that is your human endeavor.

You need not become or attain God and, even if you could become God, you'd be sorry, because if that happened, you would no longer be understood by anybody. Strive instead for one goal, and that is to understand your Self; know how to know the Self. If you do not know yourself and you are trying to know God, it is not possible to do so.

Sometimes people just shut out all these ideas of knowing themselves—they throw them away, and instead, have blind faith in God. But if you do this, your faith will waiver because it is not reasoned faith and it has not been assimilated by the mind. Your mind will always come in between you and faith. Such faith will not fully develop, because your mind will not allow you to maintain it.

As a child, I was very close to my Master, so I had a special privilege. I was very possessive of him and he was very loving to all, but he had a special love for me. One day I got angry with him. I said, "After all these years you still have not shown me God. All these great swamis come to you to learn and they go away happily, saying that they have attained something, but I have not attained anything. I don't want to be a hypocrite any more. You show me God, or I will leave you in the morning!" I was really a brat!

When I said that to him, then he said, "Tomorrow morning I will show you God." I was so excited that I could not sleep that whole night. I couldn't eat my supper; I was so excited that I was not really all there.

I said to myself, "He doesn't lie, and if he said he'd do it, then it's the truth." I asked him, "Can you tell me one thing: why didn't you show me God seventeen years ago? Why are you doing it now, after all these years?"

He replied, "You never asked to see God before, and today you asked me, so I will definitely show you God in the morning."

I could barely sleep at all the whole night; I was so restless. I said, "O Lord, let the sun rise and shine so that this morning I can go to my Master and he can show me God!"

When the morning came, I woke. In those days, I took my bath early in the morning in the cold Ganges water, even in winter. But that day I didn't feel anything. I took my bath and went to stand in front of him—excited, emotional, and completely wrecked and disorganized in my mind. That morning, I was extraordinarily devoted to him; I prostrated and bowed to him. When you live with somebody you don't observe such formalities every day. Usually, I'd say simply, "Good morning, Sir," because I was there all the time, but that day I brought him some wildflowers, and he gave me a look, and said, "What is this abnormal behavior?"

I said, "You are going to show me God."

He said, "That is why you are doing all these rituals? Okay, son, sit down. First, tell me what type of God you want to see."

I said, "Type of God? I never thought about that question! Are there types of God?"

He said, "Not really, but you must have your own concept of God, and I don't want to change your concept. You think about it and however you conceive God in your mind, whatever the picture you have in your mind about God, I will show you God according to that concept."

I said, "But, I have not yet formed any concept of God."

Then he replied, "The day you develop one, I'll show it to you."

His point was that it is our minds that create concepts like God. But the mind can never have a full concept of God, because the mind does not have such a vast capacity. God cannot be truly conceptualized by the human mind. Most of us create a limited concept of God and Guru, and later on, we find that both are actually different than what we conceived.

In my case, for seventeen years I had had a notion of God, which crumbled in five minutes' time. My master said, "Shall I show you God as it is, or do you want to see God the way you want to see Him? If I show you God as it is, you will not believe it because the picture in your mind is different, and if I show you God the way you *think* it is, that image is already there. Either way, you will not be convinced. The best way is to understand yourself first."

As you go on increasing your understanding of yourself, you will find that your "necessities" have changed. Today you think you need to have a good home, but after you increase your understanding, your needs change. Now, you think you need a good car or a woman or a good man, but that changes. Your necessities change in the process of evolution as you go on changing. Your concepts will also change. Don't hanker after God; know about yourself first. You are fully equipped to know yourself; you have all the means and tools to do so. You do not have to run around for this. You cannot honestly say, "I am not capable of knowing myself."

There is a parable in the Upanishads, in which someone asks, "How do you see? Is it because of the sunlight? When there is no sunlight, is it because of the moonlight? When there is no moonlight, then is it fire that allows you to see? When there is no fire, then what helps you see?" Even in the deepest darkness, you can see yourself. You don't see yourself through your eyes, yet you know you exist. I am talking about that which you don't see with your eyes, yet you know it is right. You don't need any proof that you exist, you don't ask people, "Am I standing here?" You know it; you are here. You don't need any evidence of that. A time will come when you will know your true Self. You don't need a swami, a book or your neighbor to tell you, "Yes, you are enlightened." To become enlightened is the human endeavor; don't stop pursuing that goal. The question is, how can this human endeavor be attained?

First, you have to eliminate your foolish ideas, because otherwise they'll create obstacles in your mind. Without knowing yourself, you seek to know God. Instead, know yourself first and then you will easily know God. Your prime duty is to know yourself, and when you know the Self of all, that is God.

How can you know the Self? Through contemplation you can first set aside your body as not being the real Self. Then, you can eliminate your senses, your prana, and then your mind, because they all change—and then what is left behind is the Self. To understand the relationship between the Self and these superficial levels, imagine a light filtered by many shades. If you throw away all those shades or filters, one by one, you will find the Light inside. From a practical viewpoint, you can see light because the real Light is already within you. You recognize the light of a light bulb, the light of the sun, the light of the moon, and the light of fire, because you have a Light within. With the help of that Light, you understand all the other lights. Yet you normally ignore your own Light and search for the sunlight outside. Know your own Light, which will help you to know and see all the other lights.

One process is external; another process is internal. You have grown up and you have seen the external world, now you have to go through an internal process. I'm not saying that the external world should be ignored; instead, the external world should be arranged and managed in such a way that it does not create obstacles for you. But the external world cannot really help you know the internal Self. Even if you use the largest telescope in the world to see the sun, moon, stars, and the entire galaxy, if you turn that telescope toward yourself, you will not see anything. Nothing external is going to help you in your quest. To see that Self, you will have to use that light that is there even when there is no light existing outside you. That is the light, knowledge, and wisdom that tell you that you exist. You have to use this light as your guide, and you need to use a particular method to do this.

If your goal is to reach the end of the earth in the East

and you spend your whole life walking, but you are walking the other direction, you will only end up in the West. At present, you are already walking, but you are walking in the wrong direction. Your human efforts should be applied in a methodical manner and then they will help you. That particular method was systematized, organized, and codified long ago by a great man named Patanjali. He systematized the method of yoga.

There have been many scholarly commentaries on the *Yoga Sutras* but all the commentaries miss something very practical. Such commentaries can only satisfy the intellect, but do not actually help you beyond that: *"yogash chitta vritti narodha"*—yoga is the control of the "modifications" of the mind. *Narodha* means control; there is no other English word for it. Control doesn't mean suppression, but channeling or regulating. You use this word everyday, just as you use many words without knowing why you are using them, resulting in confusion.

The same is true in your personal life—most of your arguments at home or elsewhere are not because you and the other person are bad people, but because you do not understand each other's language—that is why you fight. If you do not communicate well with your husband, even though he is a good man and you are also a very good person, it is because you don't understand each other's language.

Once, when Christ was speaking by the Sea of Galilee, his disciples begged him, "Master, don't speak to us in parables, because we don't understand what you are saying." Christ was on a different level spiritually than they were, and they did not understand His language. Sometimes, you are on one wavelength and your husband is on a different wavelength and you don't understand each other, although you both mean well.

To communicate with others, you have to learn to communicate first with yourself. Your external communication begins on the thought level, not through your speech or action. All your problems can be solved if you understand this point. Your communication can be bad communication or good communication; it could be frustrating or pleasant—but communication always starts on the mental level. The real point is to work with your own mind and your mental communication first.

Patanjali said that yoga means *chitta vritti narodha,* that is, having control of the mind's modifications. Control does not mean suppression. Suppression will definitely control you and affect how you lead your life—but that's not what Patanjali is saying. Many translators and commentators on the *Yoga Sutras* could not find a completely suitable word, so they used the verb "control," but this should not be understood to mean suppression.

The various faculties of mind have different dominant qualities and they work together, just as all your fingers work together. If one of your fingers is missing, it is difficult to do certain things; if two of them are missing, it is even harder—if I try to hold a glass, it may fall. Without mental understanding and coordination, nothing in your life can function well. Sometimes, even though you are brilliant and your intellect (the faculty of mind called buddhi) is wonderful, either your ego or your manas does not allow buddhi to function smoothly. Coordination of the mind's functions is very important. You need to learn how to coordinate all of these different faculties so that they work together harmoniously. In Western music, the term "harmony," refers to a way in which different notes are applied to complement each other, creating the harmony. The process you need to understand is how to allow your different mental faculties to work together to create a harmony.

In the West everything external has been systematized, but nothing internal has been systematized. In the East. everything internal has been systematized but now they are fighting to create external systems that function well. In the West, you need to balance your lives. Just as you arrange things in a neat and orderly way in the external world, so also can you arrange things in the internal world, so that the mind functions well, the buddhi functions well, the ego functions well and there is coordination and harmony within.

Presently, there are constant conflicts in the mind, and because they are not resolved, you are always emotional. Your emotional life and those unresolved problems within, constantly create conflicts for you. Those conflicts come out in anger in many ways. But there is also a definite process for resolving such conflicts, and that can be learned when you understand yourself.

There is one serious problem in modern students— they are like children! A child will plant seeds in the evening, and early the next morning he or she will wake up and start digging up the seeds to see what has happened. Of course, nothing has happened; the seeds are still there, so the child covers them up again and pours water on them. Then, in the afternoon, the child wants to examine the seeds again. Let the seeds of your practice grow; give your practice some time to develop.

The relationship between the conscious mind and the unconscious mind is very important. When you love someone, you cannot at first tell that person that you love him or her, because you are still assimilating that idea in your unconscious mind. The conscious mind knows it, but the unconscious mind does not know it, and you are still assimilating that idea in the unconscious. When your unconscious mind understands this fully, then it forces the idea to the conscious mind and then you speak of your love, and you can say, "I love you," with full confidence.

As long as there are conflicts in your mind, it means that you have not resolved certain things. Such conflict creates misery and then you experience that misery. You can resolve your conflicts yourself. No one else is going to resolve them for you. The greatest disease of all is not heart disease, strokes, cancer or any other physical disease. The greatest human disease is loneliness. In the modern world, you have all the comforts of life and you are still lonely. You have a spouse, you live under the same roof, you share the same bed, and you are still lonely. You have all experienced it. That loneliness is deep within you; it is related to the deepest level of yourself and not to external things.

Once, many years ago, a prince went to see my master at his cave retreat. The caves in the Himalayas were not holes; they were large monasteries. I was young then, and when I was young I was still very active, so I stood outside the cave. It was ten o'clock in the morning, and the prince came with all his secretaries and guards. He said, "Brahmachari, I want to see your master!"

I said, "Get out of this place! You cannot see my master!"

He thought that this boy who was speaking to him was very arrogant and irresponsible, and I said to him, "You are the one who is arrogant and irresponsible, not me!" He realized that that could be true, so then he said mildly, "Sir, can I please see your master?"

I said, "Now you can, because you are humble."

So he went inside and sat quietly. He said, "Good morning to you, sir," because he was educated at Oxford University; he could not say anything more meaningful. How is someone relating to you by saying "good morning" to you? These are the Western mantras—you say "sorry," "good morning," and "good afternoon"—but these are merely external rituals.

My master merely nodded his head. The prince said, "You seem to be lonely, sir."

My master said, "Yes, because you have come."

The prince did not understand what he meant, so my

master said, "I was enjoying the company of my great friend within, and you have come, and have made me lonely."

Consider who makes you lonely—the one whom you love or who claims to love you will make you lonely. Wanting to be in the company of someone to whom you are attached will make you lonely. You do not feel lonely because of outsiders or foreigners. The corners of your so-called love make you lonely, because your love is not always constant.

But there is someone who is always the same, always constant, opening his arms to embrace you—the greatest friend within. Everyone else will abandon you; no one else will always communicate with you. Eventually, a time comes when no one can communicate with you. You cannot speak to your wife or husband, even though she or he is prepared to help you. Your neighbor, your boss, everyone is prepared to help you, but you cannot speak to them. At the time at which everything else in life becomes hazy, who is going to help you? Only your own friend within; he will say, "I am here, why are you worried?" To establish this friendship, you have to be aware of that friend, aware that you have a friend within. Then, if you have established this friendship within, you are never lonely and you can also communicate well in the external world, because the external world is like a theatre.

In the external world, you may not really be happy but when your spouse says, "How are you, honey?," You say, "Oh, I'm very happy!" and you make certain gestures. This is all an act; you are hiding yourself, while creating conflicts within. In the external world you should learn to act well, yet also reveal yourself within; this is skillful living. This will not create a split personality. Your parents taught you to smile when you see someone, whether there is some reason to smile or not. Everyone expects you to learn this. The external world is entirely different from the internal world. To know the internal world, you have to understand yourself systematically.

I have never told any of my students to abandon his religion or his culture. I only teach you the methods which I have learned and which are verified. If you can accept them for your spiritual health, growth, and well-being, that is good. This is a system of commitment, not commandment. You are committing to yourself, to your path, and to the goal that you will know yourself. This is your commitment; it is not a commandment from outside you, that you must know yourself. If you don't want to know yourself or don't care to know yourself, then no one can force you. But as you grow you will come to a point where you will want to know your deeper Self, and then you become committed to the idea that you will know yourself in this lifetime. You want to know yourself on all levels, not just physically. You often compare your body with others and think you are different from others, but that level of observation is not the way to Truth. The mental world is far larger than the world we see outside us. If you want to analyze only five minutes of your thinking process, it will require several hours to do that; one hour takes several days.

Learn to know yourself; you have sufficient time to accomplish that. Don't use the excuse that you don't have enough time. You sometimes say, "I have not attained anything; I have been doing meditation for thirteen years!" Are you sure that you have been doing meditation? Did you sit and sleep or dream or think? For thirteen years you have been thinking about many other things in the name of meditation; you think about your work and your boyfriend or girlfriend. You sat for all those years in meditation but you did not really meditate, and then you complain that nothing has happened to you. Do not give your mind space to wander when you meditate, but go step by step in the process. First, pay attention to your posture. Do your practice systematically, learning to sit correctly. Then, work to eliminate the mental and emotional obstacles.

You are frustrated for many reasons and you place the blame on the meditation process. You should do your part, but often this is the problem—you are not fully playing your part. When the question of eating good-tasting food or another enticing distraction comes, you don't remember your meditation. At other times, when your meditation time comes and you cannot meditate, you blame the meditation itself. This is not fair; you must do things systematically. Every action has a reaction. It is not possible for you to do meditation and not receive benefits, but you may not notice those benefits now, because meditation is a conscious act, and slowly and gradually you are storing in the unconscious the *samskaras* (impressions) that will help you later. If you sow a seed today, you don't reap the fruit tomorrow, but eventually you will. It takes time to see results; be gentle with yourself. Expectation itself is a problem: you are expecting to grow a mango on a pumpkin vine, and searching for mangos on that vine where there is a pumpkin growing. Don't do anything for your teacher's sake; do your practice for yourself. The best thing that I have learned in my life is how to meditate. You should do something valuable with your life: meditate.

But on what object or focus do you meditate? The mind always wants to have something to focus on; it flies away to some picture, object, or idea. If you do your meditation systematically it is a complete process of training yourself. If you practice meditation systematically, even for only one month, it will help you. You should sit down every day at exactly the same time. Such training is very powerful. If you study soldiers, you may notice a soldier who is not particularly intelligent but has been systematically trained in some drill. In the beginning, when the instructor says "left," the soldier's right foot moves, but after some practice and training on the correct foot, no one has to say "left," he will always use that foot.

Training your mind is very important: just as you have unconsciously trained yourself in negativity, you can train yourself to be positive in your mind. This is an important point to understand; if you do something according to a specific time schedule, that regularity of time does something beneficial for your mind. Because time is a prime condition of mind, it is a great factor in strengthening your practice. If you want to learn to meditate, follow that process of establishing a specific time for your practice.

In meditation, you sometimes expect to experience foolish things—you want to see lights and colors. If you meditate with such ideas, you will never really meditate. Meditation means gently fathoming all the levels of yourself, one level after another. Be honest at least with yourself. Don't care what others say about practice—keep your mind focused on your goal. It is your own mind that does not allow you to meditate. Your untrained mind is like a garbage disposal. To work with your mind, you'll have to be patient, you'll have to work gradually with yourself.

Meditation will give you a tranquil mind. Meditation will make you aware of the Reality deep within. Meditation will make you fearless; meditation will make you calm; meditation will make you gentle; meditation will make you loving; meditation will give you freedom from fear—those are the results of meditation. If you understand these goals and want to do meditation, then it will help you, but if you are expecting to become rich through meditation, then don't do it.

The first step in meditation is concentration. Whatever you do—whether you are an accountant or a dancer—you have to be able to concentrate. If you are a musician, for example, and you can concentrate, then the more you concentrate, the more subtle your skills will become, and then the music develops and becomes very pleasing to yourself and to others. The first step in meditation is concentration, and you can attain that depth of concentration if you train yourself.

Never give up! Accept meditation as a part of your life, just as you eat, sleep, and do other things; make it a prominent goal to have a calm mind, to have a one-pointed mind, to have a tranquil mind. Do not give that up. Your meditation reflects its effect on your face. Your face is the index of your heart; meditation leaves a clear indication on your heart, which is reflected on the face. I can easily tell when a person speaks to me whether he or she meditates or not, and is capable of meditation or not.

The important theme is that you should know how to work with yourself, how to know the Self. The student must do his practice, otherwise the teacher cannot do anything. The teacher's responsibility is fifty percent; the other fifty percent is the student's. Where you encounter obstacles then the teacher will help you, but if you don't do your part and you expect the teacher to do his duty, then there's nothing anyone can do.

To become a good citizen, to become an evolved human being, to become a better follower of your own religion, or a better participant in your own culture, you have to meditate. Meditation is a neutral method; it is not a part of any particular culture. All the great men and women of wisdom meditated. Christ certainly meditated. Had he not had that wisdom of meditation and contemplation, He would have shouted, "O Romans, please help me, don't put me to death." Moses, Rama, Krishna, and all the great people were people of meditation.

Meditation establishes your conviction, and then your faith is strengthened. Then, your faith cannot be shattered or scattered by anything on the earth. This is the process of training yourself.

You all remain influenced by the fear of death. You are afraid of death because you see other people dying, even though you do not experience death in your own daily life. Consider this question: what do you know about death? You do not really understand death. Such fears remain unresolved within your mind. Then, you are terrified and full of fear. Outside, you wear a beautiful dress and have a beautiful face and you are smiling, but inside you are terrified, and your behavior shows that. You do not walk freely; you don't walk like the Lord of the earth. You don't feel that the earth is meant for you, that it is given to you to enjoy. Whenever you walk, you walk in fear. You walk as if you are dead, as if someone has the strings and is pulling you, and you are forced to live in the world. How did Christ live and walk on the earth? He was born to death in the same way that we are born to die. He became great because He made a human effort. The divine grace will come of itself; the divine wisdom will come itself if you have made your human endeavor.

When your desires are not fulfilled, you get angry; unfulfilled desire leads to anger. When you get angry with someone, it is because he or she is not fulfilling your desires. You are not satisfied with him or her, and you become angry. In this fashion you get angry a thousand times a day, because there are so many expectations in your mind. A desire creates expectation, and that longing or expectation is strong, so there is constant anger. When you express your anger it wrecks your nervous system. You start trembling when you are angry; you lose your balance; you lose your tranquility.

Learning to live in the world—the technique of living in the world yet remaining above the world—that's what you need to develop. Don't waste your time thinking or expecting too much of the world. The world can only give you a little bit; it hasn't got much to give you. You expect too much from the world and then you weep with disappointment. The world says, "I'm sorry, I cannot really give you what you want." Unfortunately, you don't listen to that other whisper from within, the whisper of the Self, that Source which can answer your desires.

Chapter 2

Positive Living
and the Transformation of
Your Habit Patterns

In the East, when we bring our hands together in a gesture of greeting and respect, it reminds us that the individual soul meets the Cosmic Soul, and we acknowledge the reality, "Thou art That." We bring our hands together in respect because it symbolizes the place where these two meet.

There's another reason why we bring our hands together. This gesture also reminds us that the internal and external worlds must be brought into balance in order to make life successful, and to fulfill the purpose of life.

The knowledge that I have received in the course of my life is from the great sages and their sayings, and of course, I have also observed the way you people live—both in the East and West. After visiting hundreds of countries I have discovered that all over the world there is one great problem, and that problem is that the human being has not yet understood himself or herself, and tries, instead, to understand God and others. As we discussed earlier, you often try to analyze others without first understanding yourself. You become very judgmental when you talk about others; whatever trait you dislike, you project it onto others and then say, "This person is like that." You form the habit of projection and it continues on and on, and it limits your growth throughout your life, because as long as you project onto others you do not ever see yourself clearly.

Your habit patterns have a very powerful role in your life and a strong influence on your spiritual development. Once you understand how to form habit patterns, you can then understand the path of positive living. In America, people always smile publicly. This pattern is taught during your childhood, and when I first visited New York, I had a problem because of it. When I left my hotel, I wanted to cross the street, and everyone was making this strange facial gesture at me. I wondered if something was wrong with my clothes, so I went back to my hotel room and changed my clothes, and put on the best suit I had. But again, when I went out the door, someone came and made that expression at me. Finally, I stopped someone on the street and said, "Why are you making this face at me?"

He said, "Sir, we are taught to smile at others in this country." I said, "But this is not smiling!" Such social behavior has become your nature. When you see someone, you do that and then you become serious again. Your culture teaches you to smile at others, but such smiles are only momentary and do not reflect your real feelings.

Actually, there should be a perennial and real smile on your face all the time. To achieve that, you need to have a clear concept about the meaning of life. You should understand something about life and the deeper philosophy of life. It's actually a simple philosophy, and once you understand it and are familiar with that philosophy, then you will start functioning on a different and deeper level, and you will begin to enjoy your life.

Such an enjoyment does not mean merely enjoying something momentarily. Regardless of all that you have or don't have, within and without, you can enjoy life, provided you have the right philosophy. Life is a manuscript, and the author of that manuscript is that which you are.

Life is not a book written by someone else; all individuals are the authors of the manuscript that they are; that's life.

The beginning and the ending of this manuscript are missing. You do not consciously know from where you have come; you do not know where you will go. But you have the middle portion of the manuscript with you, and if you do not study that middle portion of the manuscript which you are, you will never search for and succeed in retrieving the missing pages of your life's manuscript.

This is a very interesting subject to study. Studying books can give you some solace in life, but I don't listen much to those who merely study books all the time. I say, "If you study books all the time, when do you practice and when do you think?" and they have no answer for me.

You should learn to study the greatest of all books, and that is life itself. You are the creator of your own destiny. No one else creates problems, miseries or pains for you, not even God. God is the center of equality and love, so why should God be partial, and make one person happy and another unhappy? That doesn't make any sense; whatever human beings experience, they think it is the result of God's will, but God does not make anyone unhappy. Happiness or unhappiness is your own creation.

Without understanding life itself, you will not understand your own habit patterns, and then you will never really enjoy life. To live is a grace from Providence, but to live happily is of your own making.

Human beings cannot live without doing some actions. Your actions are very different from the actions of animals. In the animal kingdom, we can observe that the activities of animals are basically controlled and governed by nature. But human beings are not totally governed by nature; you have conquered nature. You have a brain, you have a mind, and you have many faculties of mind, such as buddhi, or intelligence. Your wisdom tells you that if it's raining, you can take a coat, or use an umbrella, or make a shelter.

The human being is the finest of all species, and there is no creature known so far that is higher than human beings. Even *devas,* which are called "bright beings" or angels, aspire to be human beings. You are the way you are because you *wanted* to be the way you are. And you can become the way you want to be. Don't postpone your improvement and enlightenment by saying, "Well, whatever God has created, I accept it." That is merely inertia or laziness—which is a sin.

I don't really believe in such a thing as sin; sin merely means inertia. Sin means only that you're constantly hurting or harming yourself, or that you're not improving yourself. It means that you're not exploring the deeper dimensions of your life, or understanding your internal states. Sin means you are not evolving or attaining the next step of life.

Throughout your life you have done experiments on matter, mind, and energy, but you have not done enough experiments on the real Self within you. You've merely been repeating the word, "God," and just as your ancestors died, you will also leave your bodies—nothing new or different is going to happen.

I am telling you to face this reality: the path to enlightenment and unfoldment is not really so austere, abstruse, or difficult—it's actually very easy. The easiest way to make progress is just to "know thyself"—to accept and understand yourself on all levels. To know yourself you don't need external crutches; you don't need gurus or teachers to know yourself. Once you know the way, become aware of the goal, and have determination, then it's easy for you to understand yourself. You have every right to understand and enlighten yourself.

You do not need such happiness that comes for a mere moment and then, after a few seconds, makes you unhappy for minutes or hours. Happiness is that which is everlasting. Happiness is that which elevates you, that which you can share with others. You have formed a bad habit of sharing your grief and sorrows with others, but you do not share your real happiness with others, because you do not know what it is, although it exists within. What good are the objects that you attain in the external world, if you do not explore the inner dimensions of life? Since your childhood you have been taught to see and examine things in the external world, but no one has ever taught you how to look within, see within, and discover within.

The one important part of life is ignored by your educational systems at home, in society, and in the colleges and universities: "Know thyself." You need to understand yourself on all levels. When you really understand yourself, you'll no longer experience such problems as divorce. At your present state, you say to someone, "I like you. I love you, honey," and the next day you get married, and after a week the relationship falls apart. You are both good people, but you don't understand each other, and that is creating chaos in your society. It is the children who are suffering the most. Those children become wild; they do not become good citizens; there is violence and more violence. There is no real communication in your culture. Human beings do not understand each other, and it all comes down to one point: bad training in early childhood.

You often raise this question: "Our childhoods are gone, and they will not return in this lifetime; is there any way that we can still improve ourselves?" The answer is that you can definitely improve and grow once you become aware of the fact that you are fully responsible for your actions.

The first real step of development in life is to know yourself, not to talk about knowing God. But how do you know yourself? So far, you have learned about yourself mainly through your body. You are a physical being, but knowing this level is not enough for you to understand yourself fully. You are also a breathing being, a sensing being, and a thinking being. All this takes place because you are that Center of Consciousness within, from where Consciousness flows on various degrees and grades.

This path to which I'm introducing you, and the journey of which I am making you aware, is a journey within. You are trying to explore who you are, so that you can function well in your life, understand your habit patterns, and learn to live happily in the world. To learn that, you don't need to go to church or study books, but rather, to study your own self on three levels: action, speech, and mind. Any discipline you learn is meant to help you improve on these three dimensions—action, speech, and mind.

Life is a mystery, and it can be analyzed in many different ways. A poet analyzes this mystery in one unique way, an intellectual in another, and a logician in a still different way. Religionists simply say, "Do not analyze anything, just believe in God," but it's not easy to believe in God without fully understanding and experiencing what that concept means.

One person wants to visualize God on the cross, another on the Mount, another in front of a burning bush, and another imagines God playing a flute. You form your own concepts of God, and you become hypnotized by the sayings and writings of others. That's how you live, and then such a person, who has merely known God through the sayings of others, is considered to be holy. If God appeared in front of you, you would not know what to do with Him. If Jesus came to America, Americans would put him behind bars, even though you talk of Him all the time.

Vedanta philosophy says that you first need to be de-hypnotized, that you need to understand free thinking. Free thinking will come when you fully understand all the faculties of mind and the modifications of your mind, when you understand each part of the whole wheel of the mind separately. I don't want to shatter your understanding or concept of God. I know I am telling you something that is hard to understand, but I have to, because otherwise you will not make any progress on the path.

There was once a swami who used to teach students every day. One of the students listened attentively and heard the swami speaking about *vairagya,* the philosophy of non-attachment, and the student took off for a forest dwelling and there, he was enlightened.

After dwelling there for twelve years, he wondered what had happened and what had been the fate of his friends, with whom he used to learn. So he returned to that place, and everyone was still sitting there exactly like before, and the swami was still lecturing. What a waste of time! The point is that you don't need much external information; you already have true knowledge within. You need to learn how to apply the knowledge that you have. You are taught: "Be good, be nice, be gentle, be loving." You have all been taught that, but you should learn to practice, understand, and to apply that knowledge to yourself.

You need to understand how you function, and the process that results in your actions. There is an important difference between an animal and a human being: the activities of animals are controlled by nature, but that's not the case with human beings.

The *Bhagavad Gita,* one of the major texts of India, contains the essence of the *Vedas* and *Upanishads,* and it describes the importance of human actions: "O, human being, you can attain perfection by doing your own actions skillfully." This is acuniversal law: "As you sow, so shall you reap"—whatever a tions you perform, they have their consequences. There is no "forgiveness" in this law at all: it is simply a matter of cause and effect. No matter how many gods come down and forgive you, if you sow an apple seed, the tree will not give you pears. No matter how many times you pray for pears, it's not going to happen. Your prayers are a waste of time and energy because it is your actions that determine what you experience.

Most of the time, your prayers are childlike prayers, like those of a child who constantly asks his mother, "Give me this, give me that," all day long. This kind of prayer makes you a beggar, and a beggar can never meet His Majesty, the King of kings. In order to meet the King of kings and the Lord of life—the One whom you call God—you have to *be* God. But without knowing yourself, you cannot be God.

First, you must learn to deal skillfully with your actions. Whatever action you perform, you do so because you have assumed that action as your duty. Action has no meaning if it is not done as a part of your duty. It becomes a part of your duty because you have assumed it as a duty and accepted it as such. You assume certain duties as a member of a particular family, and then you perform the actions that follow from those duties.

This next aspect is important to understand: when you perform any action, you are bound to reap the fruits of your actions. That's a scientific law: every action has it's reaction, so every action you perform will give you a particular kind of fruit or consequence.

The fruits of those actions will then again motivate you to perform more actions, and from morning until evening, endlessly, throughout your whole life, and up to the last breath of your life, you continue to act. There is no end to this process of action and consequences—it becomes a whirlpool for you, and you cannot come out of it. You are caught in this whirlpool: you cannot live without performing actions. A human being is bound to perform certain actions simply because he's a human being. This is the way your habits are formed: one day you perform a particular action, and the next day, your memory of that experience leads you to perform that action again and again. Thus, it becomes a repetition. The more you repeat something over and over, the more it creates a great, deep groove in your mind, and then that eventually becomes a habit.

Perhaps you think, "Oh, my habit is only a superficial one, I can stop drinking anytime," because you have not been drinking alcohol for a long time. But sometimes when you examine a habit you realize, "I've been drinking for a long time; it's very difficult for me to stop drinking now." But even so, you can change your behavior; you can definitely free yourself from the bondage of such addictions, if you decide and firmly resolve, "I need help." There are people in the world who can help you if you really want help. Your problem is not a sin, it's only a bad habit. If you really examine yourself closely you will realize that your habits *are* your personality—that they have *created* your personality. Your personality has been woven by your habit patterns, and your habit patterns are your repetitive actions. No action can ever be performed unless you think or want it on some level of the mind, so your habits and personality are a reflection of that level.

For example, if you don't even think of going in a certain direction, you will never end up there. The real motivation for each action is your thought. But there is something even more powerful beneath the thought level, and that is the emotional power within you, a deeper part of your mental process. Emotion is very powerful, and if you can use that emotional power, you can attain the highest state of ecstasy in a second's time. But if you mingle and blend that emotional power with your negative habit patterns, then you are gone! Then, no one can protect you from yourself. An immense resource is within you, but it is either not being utilized by you at all, or is being badly utilized. You presently use your emotional power to form bad habit patterns.

How do you tell which habit patterns are bad and which are good? Negative habit patterns are those injurious to your health on all levels—physical, mental, and spiritual. Good habit patterns are healthy and helpful to you. There are two categories of objects described in the *Upanishads: shreyas* and *preyas*. Preyas means that which is pleasant, and shreyas means that which is helpful. Sometimes pleasant experiences or things are not really at all helpful to you. Sometimes, too, that which is very helpful is not at all pleasant to you, especially at first, because of your negative habit patterns. You have to understand what is really good for you, what is truly helpful for you. If I ask someone, "Please don't eat sugar," or, "Please don't be cross to your husband," the person may reply, "I love him, but what can I do, I'm just cross," or, "I can't stop eating sugar." The person knows that her husband is a wonderful man and she loves him very much, but when she eats sugar, it agitates her system and then she becomes cross and harsh with him.

This is a habit. You know that you are hurting yourself through such behavior, so don't look for a cause outside yourself. Nothing is going to help you if you do not decide to help yourself. When you decide to help yourself—when a human being determines to improve himself—then Providence also helps him. If you help yourself to be sick, Providence will allow you to do that, but if you help yourself to be healthy, then Providence says, "I will supply all that you need to recharge your battery."

You should never give up in working with yourself. One thing that is very destructive in life is to weaken your own willpower. Your willpower says, "I can do it; I will do it; I have to do it!" This is what you should always remind yourself: "I can do it; I will do it, and I have to do it!"

If you fail and stumble once, try again; don't give up. Giving up is defeat, and that defeat will cripple your inner sensitivity and then you will lose that sensitivity. Try to work with yourself. Correct practice will lead you to perfection—work with yourself. If you talk too much, for example, then decide that you will continue to speak and do so purposefully, but not uselessly. Those who speak too much usually speak nonsense. They don't say what they really want to say. You waste your energy through your speech, and this is also the case with your actions—you waste your energy by performing actions that are injurious for your health and your future.

But you should never give up, because there are many examples of those who have transformed themselves and made great changes in their personalities. There was once a great sage in India whose name was Valmiki. He was originally a robber, and took delight in robbing swamis and sages. One day a swami was going down the path and that swami did not own anything but a water pot. Valmiki captured the swami, snatched his water pot, and beat him. The swami said, "Son, listen to me first, and then you can beat me up or kill me! Why are you doing this? Do you think you are doing it for your wife or children? Why have you formed such a bad habit?"

The same thing happened with Saint Paul. Before he became a great spiritual leader, Saint Paul was Saul, a very bad man. He was transformed on the way to Damascus, because his conscience began to ask him questions: "Why are you doing these things? Why aren't you walking on the path of righteousness?" And because he listened to his conscience, he transformed himself.

Many times, whether or not we human beings are educated and cultured, our conscience comes forward and asks us, "Why are you doing all this?" You don't need anyone outside yourself to tell you that something is right or wrong for you; you know it!

When you repeatedly do something, it becomes an addiction. You know that the behavior is bad, yet you continue to do it. Nothing has clouded your power of knowing or your knowledge, but you have to learn to practice and apply what you know. When I ask you why you aren't sitting regularly for your meditation, many of you wonder why a swami from India has come to your country and is teaching something that is not fully accepted by your culture or traditions.

I remind you that your ancient teachers knew how to meditate, but you have forgotten. You have become dissipated; you have forgotten yourself in the rush of external stimuli. You've gone far away from yourself. Come home, or you will only succeed in creating a huge asylum in the world.

These days, a human being has all the imaginable comforts, but he's still not at all happy. He has no anchor in life; he has nothing to hold on to and he is full of fear and misery. You are all so serious and no one seems to know how to truly smile. That's why I suggest that you meditate. Learn to be quiet for a few minutes every day, so that the knowledge from the infinite library within you can come forward and make you aware that the purpose of life is not merely to earn an external living. These external means are meant to make you comfortable and secure, so that you can attain the highest purpose of life. One part of your task is already over; you have attained one part of life—the external means—but beyond that, you have not yet attained anything.

The next step is to learn to discriminate whether the means that you have are really helpful to you or not. The means that you have should be helpful in such a way that they don't create other pain or discomfort. But actually, no external means will ever help you to attain real wisdom, the height of perfection. These means have their limited sphere, but you will have to search within yourself, and find the real wisdom within yourself.

Sometimes a person who has no home and very few things is very happy; but you have everything and you're still not happy. Why do renunciates who have so little seem to be happy, while householders do not? A householder should be happier than a renunciate, because renunciates live on the charity of householders. You should create a clear philosophy of life for yourself—you think all the time, but you don't yet have a clear philosophy. Your philosophy should start with an understanding of your duties, the duties that you have assumed in life. You cannot live without doing your duties, so what will you do? Will you retire, run away, and escape from those duties? Where will you go? Wherever you go, you will have to do something.

Actually, a householder's life is superior to any other way of life, yet it seems that a funny thing is happening in the world: Rishikesh is a city at the foot of the mountains in the Himalayas, and the Ganges flows through there. From the mountainside I can see the other side of the river, and the people on the other side can see my side. Those who are sitting on one side are thinking: "Oh, what a wonderful place the Himalayas are! If we go there we will become great sages." And the people in the Himalayas think about what people are doing in New York! Householders think, "Oh, how well these priests, sages, swamis, and yogis live. They are the happiest people on the earth," but the yogis are thinking, "What are we going to eat tomorrow? We don't have anything!"

You don't need to make any external change to improve your inner situation: be wherever you are. Learn to decide things and to create determination, and you can attain the highest state. You'll never become lost if you search within, but you'll always be lost if you are searching for something outside yourself. The search lies within, from the gross self to the subtlest aspect of your being.

Certainly, you should realize that you have a body, and it is a useful instrument, so you should keep it healthy. But the body will not lead you to enlightenment. When you raise your identification from the level of the body, then there will be no pain in the body. Don't ever let yourself be terrified by death, for death is merely a part of life. Death is sure to come, and it is never painful. What is painful is the *fear* of death. To fear, "I will die! I will die!" is certainly painful, but death itself is not painful. Even the healthiest person dies, the wealthiest dies, the richest dies, and the poorest dies. Death itself is not painful; that which is painful is thinking about death, because it is a negative way of thinking.

If you observe yourself, you will notice that you are negative most of the time. For example, a wife may worry because her husband has not come home on time. Perhaps he usually comes home at nine o'clock, and today it's already ten-thirty and he has not come back yet. If she doesn't know how to manage her fears and her thinking, and how to take such a thing, she may telephone the police station or the hospitals, or she may get worried and disturb the neighbors and wake up the children—all because of her negative and fearful thinking.

You remain negative and frightened all the time: you are afraid of dying, you are afraid of not attaining what you want, and you are afraid of losing what you have. You have so many fears, and fear is the greatest of all enemies.

Often, two people are afraid of each other, and so they don't communicate. You talk of security in your marital life but what security do you really experience? You feel fear; you are afraid of each other. You are afraid of each other because you don't know yourself. You each do not know yourself and yet you claim to love each other, and this is such an artificial thing! You are lying to each other and you both know it: how can you create a successful, healthy marital life when you do not know yourself and you fear each other?

You should develop some understanding of life. You usually think about others and analyze what others are doing, just like a drunken person. The similarity between you and a person who is drunk is that if the drunk is nude and sees somebody else walking along, the drunk will say,

"Hey, you nude man!" The drunk is nude himself, but he doesn't notice or become aware of that; instead he looks at others and sees the problem there.

Such is the case with most people; you criticize each other and waste your time and energy analyzing each other's faults, but you don't observe within yourself, because you are drunk. You are intoxicated and hypnotized by the suggestions of others. Others tell you, "You are like this; you are like that," and you accept such suggestions and then become what they have told you. The day that you learn to see yourself independently, you'll be free from that hypnosis, and then you will follow the path of Self-realization. That is the important difference between the processes of self-hypnosis and Self-Realization.

This path toward Self-Realization starts with work: do your duties. My duty towards my students is to teach them selflessly. If I do not do my duty well, then my conscience will create an inner conflict and I will torment myself. Such conflict within is the source of your misery, especially when you feel conflicts about how you perform your duties.

First, understand your duties and how to perform them skillfully. This is a very simple formula, but you need to apply it practically and systematically. Decide every morning that no matter what happens, you will not let anything disturb you. If you become emotionally disturbed, then you cannot do anything worthwhile.

I once knew of someone who won a lottery. He was a poor man and he got very excited about winning and then he died. You don't need that sort of happiness or joy! You don't need that sort of emotional upheaval for yourself. You need to be balanced; decide every morning that no matter what happens you will be not be emotionally disturbed, and that you will deal with the things that come. If you resolve to do this, you'll find that a great change takes place in your life.

You should study and fully understand the law of

action or karma. Whatever you do, you are bound to receive and reap the fruits of your actions. Then, since those fruits again motivate you to further action, there is no end to the process. You can never emerge from or escape that process, but there is a path to freedom— freedom from the bondage of your actions and karma.

You cannot renounce performing these karmas. You have to do even what you call your daily duties: caring for your body, eating food, and going to the bathroom. So there is no such thing as total renunciation of action. Learning to live on the earth, to live in the world and yet remain unaffected and above it is your goal. Renunciation alone is not the path. There is a kind of conquest on your path: your path is to live in the world yet remain unaffected by worldly fetters; this should be your determination every morning. Often, you weaken yourself in daily life: you leave for work smiling and then suddenly something happens on your way to work and you become sad. That's life: you are constantly experiencing the changes and the ups and downs of life, all the time. To deal with these changes, you must develop your determination that you will not be emotionally disturbed by events, and will not do anything that hurts or harms those with whom you live.

You often talk about love, but you cannot really define love. Many years ago, when I first visited this country, I asked a boy in San Diego, "What does it mean to love thy neighbor as thyself?"

He replied, "It means that if you find a good looking girl as one of your neighbors, run away with her." Such ideas are the result of cultural habit patterns. He was never taught what real love means. I called his parents and I asked, "What are you teaching your son?" and they replied, "He's impossible! He's a teenager and we cannot do anything with him!" But actually, children can be trained very easily, provided you pay attention to the early education of the child. You should pay careful attention to their training and development from early childhood: a tender bamboo shoot can be bent and trained easily, but not a mature bamboo stalk—then, the bamboo will break. Childhood is the ideal period for self-training, but even later in life, you can always improve yourself.

These days, "stress" seems to be a burning topic; everywhere you find references to stress, stress management, and stress reduction. But, what is the real cause of stress? Your neighbors, family, and work do not create stress for you. Actually, stress results either when you feel that you are doing something that you should not do, or you feel that you are being forced to do what you are doing. Stress also results when you are not able to do what you *want* to do, and that creates a conflict in your mind—that is stress. This principle applies to how you feel about food, sex, sleep, and your need for self-preservation. Everyone feels that life is stressful, but you paint yourself up and try to look nice, and thus, everyone has a mask they use to hide how they really feel. That adds to the stress.

I remember a situation in Minneapolis, where a boy courted a girl for seven years. He said to me, "Swamiji, that girl is so beautiful. I cannot live without her. She is very beautiful."

But I said, "No, don't marry her," because I felt that his concept of love was not mature.

One day he visited her early in the morning and she had not yet put on her makeup. He suddenly thought that she was ugly and had a revulsion toward her, and came and knocked on my door at six-thirty in the morning, when I meditate.

He said, "May I come in? I don't want to marry her any more. She's ugly!" After seven years, his appreciation and admiration of her beauty was gone in one second's time. The poor girl was sleeping; she got up and went to the door when someone knocked, and then he didn't want to marry her. I told him, "I pity the depth of your love. Do you love only cosmetics? If so, then go to some cosmetic company and love that company!" This is the depth of your society's understanding of love.

We try to look nice for others, but we are actually cheating them—we try to present ourselves as something that we are not. It's good to dress nicely, to have a good haircut, and to wear nice clothes, but you have gone far away from your inner reality in every phase of your life. Your unreal behavior is reflected in your mind, action, and speech.

What I am saying is that you should learn to understand your own actions first. You have not yet observed your mind, and that's a little difficult, but first observe your actions. What are you doing? You say, "I don't want to do this, but I am doing it," or "I want to sit down, relax, have a cup of tea, and talk to you, but I cannot." This is how you create conflict and division in your own mind.

Every time you think that you want to do something but you cannot, it creates pressure within you, because you do not yet know how to love your duties. You feel that your duties are forced on you, and you do not know how to create love for your duties. You do your duties as a mere chore, without loving them, and it is *that* which creates problems for you, and makes you a slave. What you need to learn is to create love for your duties.

Sometimes you live together with someone for a long time, and you start to feel a great gap between the two of you. You don't communicate, you become angry, and perhaps you think of divorcing each other. But instead, you should learn to understand each other. This pattern of divorce is very injurious to the whole of society. It may be good or pleasant for you as one single individual, but don't forget that you are part of the larger society. Don't become a negative example to your children. If a marriage is impossible—if two negative elements came together and got married—then I am not against divorce. But why have you allowed divorce to become a custom? It is creating enormous problems for you, and you'll all face the same music of wrath in your society.

You should learn to love and not resent your duties, but what is that kind of love? You can learn to love by understanding one concept, and that is *ahimsa*. In the *Yoga Sutras* there are ten commitments. They are not commandments, but if you are committed to this path and decide to practice them, they will help you a great deal. The first step to practice, before all the other teachings, is ahimsa or "non-harming." Before you can know Truth you have to learn ahimsa, or how to love. Before you can lead a joyous life and live positively in the world, you have to learn love. But you don't even know what love means! You think that love means giving someone a cup of tea and then receiving two in return. Love really means giving—giving without any condition, constantly giving selflessly. Whenever you are truly selfless in life, then you'll enjoy life. When you are not selfless, then the expectation that prompts or motivates you to give, will actually create problems for you—tnat is not love. The difference between lust and love is that love means selfless action; lust means having expectations.

When you learn to "grease" and oil your duties with love, then life flows smoothly. All your actions should be greased by love. If you serve your husband with love, and your husband serves you and the children with love, then there will be no problems in life. Your nervous system will not be agitated, and you won't do things that you resent. Instead, you'll be happy all the time, because you are doing your duties with love.

You should also understand another point: there is a great "catch" in the world. When you talk of liberation, emancipation, and freedom, that's only a cry for help. You are creating actions and reaping the fruits of these actions, so how can you become free from this process? This is the many-runged ladder of death and birth. You do an action because you cannot live without it, and then you reap the fruit. You are miserable because you are grasping and holding onto the fruits of your actions—you are selfish and possessive. That's why you are miserable! When you learn to give to others, then you'll be free.

Giving is actually a natural part of life; it will liberate you. It's important to learn to give to your own people, those with whom you live. Learn to give spontaneously in your mind, action, and speech: that is your first step to freedom. This first step of freedom is attained when you learn to do your actions with love and learn to give. If you do not seek to do this, then you are being selfish and negative. A negative person is very selfish; a positive person is very generous. You cannot rely upon a negative person. There are some people who never come into contact with their positive emotions—they only remain negative all the time, because they lie to themselves and thus are unable to give to others.

One day, I stood at the gate of a hospital, and watched every patient coming in or going out. Those who went in were definitely sick, but those who were going home were also not perfectly healthy. I stood there and I asked them, "How are you?", and everyone said, "Fine!" Then I replied, "If you are fine, then why are you going to the hospital?" At first I thought that those people were lying, but actually they were not lying. They were only following a custom: you always say, "Fine," when somebody asks you how you are.

Don't behave in such a manner; don't become a hypocrite or be dishonest. Try to show and express that which you are. If you feel good and accepting of yourself, that's good, but if you do not feel good or accepting, don't be sad about it. Even at home, you are not completely honest with your husband when he asks how you are. When you are not honest, you create a division within yourself. You form a bad habit: you become weak and full of fear, you make yourself insecure. But life is meant to be a poem and a song, why don't you enjoy it? Every second of life should be enjoyed! The enjoyment of the past is gone, and the enjoyment in the future is only an imagination, so learn to enjoy life here and now!

You should also have the determination, "Whatever I do today, I will dedicate the fruits of my actions to those with whom I live." Love means non-harming, so you should resolve that you will not harm, hurt or injure your spouse, children, or friends—that means that you love them. The expression of your love is in not harming or hurting others. Love does not consist of telling someone that you love them and cannot live without them—that is mere selfishness. If you love someone, then don't harm or hurt them—that is the real expression of your love.

If you want to live positively and joyfully, learn to give the fruits of your actions to others, and determine that you will not allow yourself to be bothered by anything in the external world.

How are you going to enlighten yourself if you remain caught up in a whirlpool that you are creating for yourself? Most of your miseries and the experiences that you think are painful are actually created by you, and then you ask God to help you. But if you create misery for yourself, what kind of God will come down and help you? It will never happen, because that misery is being created by you.

There is a Sanskrit saying, "If you help yourself, God will help you. But if you do not help yourself, God is not going to help you." The ocean is full of water, and you can draw out as much water as you want. There's light everywhere, and nature is everywhere in abundance. You can use the power of nature according to your own needs. You have all the power you need. You simply have to be conscious; you have to be aware of who you are. Becoming free from the bondage of karma is the first step toward freedom. The second step toward freedom is to develop peaceful living in your daily life.

Married life is like a cart with two wheels, and each wheel helps the other to roll along the path. When you cannot help yourself, there is someone to help you. This gives you time to think and to improve yourself. The single life is not as good because it is not complete—you have to do everything for yourself. Two people can adjust to each other and share their duties—that creates enough time for spiritual practice. That time should be utilized for the next step, Self-Realization. That's why people get together: people do not come together only to create children, people come together so that they can share and understand each other. They help each other, and then they have enough time to seek Self-Realization.

It is not that the single life is lonely; even when you get married you are lonely! Everyone is lonely. Loneliness is the greatest of all killers, but that's not the point. Loneliness will go away only when you are Realized. Loneliness will not go away if you merely share the same roof with someone, whether or not you get married. The purpose of life is to attain a state of freedom from all misery and pain. That state is not given to you by God—it's a human creation and attainment.

The spiritual concept of marriage and home is that you should make that home and marriage a happy one, so that it radiates your happiness to others. We will discuss the process of how to accomplish this in a later chapter. Your love should go beyond the boundaries of culture, religion, and country, and should include the entire universe. That's why the great sages say, "The whole universe is our home. We are all friends."

The day that you learn to love all and exclude none, that is the day of your enlightenment. If you are waiting for enlightenment in your next life, then I have nothing to teach you—you can wait, but you'll be very sorry. You'll come back and do the same thing over again. Do not postpone your enlightenment. You can attain that enlightenment here and now, and the first step is positive living: learn not to be negative. The first step to freedom comes when you learn to do your actions with love and learn to give. When you understand your real responsibility in life, you'll know that every human being is responsible to make his life happy and then to emanate that happiness to others.

When you begin to work with your emotions you should be systematic. First, discover why you become emotional. The cause of emotion is never from deep within you; the cause of your emotions is always a reaction to things from without. Something happens externally and then you become emotional, angry or sad.

Thus, the origin of emotion is not truly from within, but from outside. There is some situation outside yourself, and when you react to it, that makes you emotional. You become emotional because you have not yet correctly arranged or understood your relationships with the external world.

If you are a little child and I hit you, you will cry, but if you hit me I won't cry, because I am strong. When you are strong, nothing external will disturb you. When something disturbs you, you should know that it is because you are weak. Understand that you are being disturbed by others because you are weak, no matter what the cause is. Examine your own strength and consider how strong you are: are you strong enough to take all the blows of life? You should decide to become strong in order to live. Learn to be strong; developing strength from within is very important.

To have real strength, learn to understand your habit patterns. Anything you do repeatedly creates a subtle groove in your unconscious mind, and then you don't have control over it any longer. Only by consciously creating a new groove will your mind begin to flow toward that new groove and then you'll improve. Then, you can consciously create new grooves in your mind. The day that you become aware that you are the master of your actions will be a great day for you. Before you are aware of this, you merely are a slave to your own mind. This awareness is important!

Never give up in the face of your own weaknesses. Never think that you cannot do something because you are a woman, for example, or that you are all alone, so you cannot do something. This is negative thinking! Don't do that to yourself. Do your best and then surrender all your actions and the fruits therein to the Almighty, the Lord of Life. Pray to Him, to the Innermost Dweller within yourself: "Give me strength so that I can endure this. Give me strength so that I am successful. Give me strength so that I don't forget You." If you ask for that, you'll gain strength. All the strength really comes from within; the outside world inspires, but strength comes from within.

It is good to share positive feelings; it is good to be cheerful with others, provided that you really have that feeling. But if you don't have cheerfulness, how can you share that with others? Of course, you don't want to share your sorrow with another person or upset others, but forming a habit of acting happy when you are not is like constantly not telling others what is real or the truth. That creates a bad habit and then becomes a part of your life. In this way, you never become aware of your real feelings. If you want to be positive without being dishonest, there's another way: you can easily say, "Things will improve," or "God will help us," or many other pleasant phrases which will not hurt others, but don't say that you are fine when you are not. This is a social habit we form. You should share your joy and cheerfulness, but that joy should not come though an artificial smile. When you smile like that, it is like slapping your cheeks and then smiling. You should have a genuine smile.

If you want to change your personality and are following a true path, and you commit a mistake, you'll receive help because of your quest of truth and righteousness. Your inner world is larger and more powerful than the world you see around you: there is something great inside you. Someone is witnessing your actions, speech, and mind, and that observer is actually you, the finest part of your Self. The day that you go to that level, you will no longer condemn yourself. Then, you'll no longer find any weakness in yourself. Go there and find that Self within. Don't continue to remain lost outside yourself and ignorant of your true and inherent nature.

Chapter 3

Perfecting
The Personality

Everyone is eager to know more about the path of spirituality. You long to know more, but there is actually a barrier that you create for yourselves, and that barrier is *practice*. You do not practice what you already know. You really do not need to know many things, but you definitely need to practice what you know. It is a sad thing to tell you, but I have not really learned anything new since I grew up; that which I learned in my childhood is what I have been practicing.

It is the same with most of you: the basic knowledge that is imparted by your parents, schools, and universities still remains unpracticed. You do not practice what you know, but you should begin to do that, so that your personality can be modified and developed.

As we discussed earlier, the word "personality" comes from its Greek root, *persona,* or mask. The Greeks used many masks in their theater. You all have and wear many masks. But who made those masks for you? They were not created by your society, culture, religion or Providence— you chose them. You are what you are; this is your choice. You wanted to be the way you are and that is how you have created yourself, so you should not blame others for your personality or its conflicts.

Plato and other Western philosophers also held the principle that you are your own creation, rather than the result of what God or Providence wants you to be. When you suffer, you sometimes think that your suffering is due to God, but that is a poor philosophy, because God never wants anyone to suffer. God is a symbol of love, the highest principle. Why would God be interested in creating suffering? Rather, it is your own actions that make you suffer. Your actions can be divided into three classes: past, present, and future.

To understand these three types of action, imagine someone carrying a quiver of arrows on his shoulder. There is one set of arrows that he has already sent toward the target—they are the actions of the past. Those arrows that he is holding in his hands are the present actions, and those arrows still in his quiver are the future actions. Perhaps you are not happy with some event from your past; perhaps you expected too much of yourself. Then you condemn yourself by thinking that you have not done enough, and you constantly repeat the thought that your past actions were not healthy or good. Thus, you have created a habit of condemning yourself, which creates negativity in your mind. But the present and future actions are still completely in your hands, and that is where you should focus your mind.

You have the power to change the destiny of your life. You have the power to change your personality. You have the power to mold the entire stream of your life, to give a new direction to your life. There is one difficulty in doing this, however, and that is your habit patterns. Your personality is a particular character, woven by your habit patterns, but how are your habits themselves formed? As we said earlier, habits are formed because you have repeated some action or thought again and again. Thus, it becomes a habit. Then, you unconsciously do it; eventually, it is a full-fledged habit. When you understand that all your habits are formed by the simple process of repeating some action or thought again and again, then you can learn another process, that of undoing and changing your habits.

I often find that in the schools and colleges, the children are taught in a very harsh and critical way. That is why they do not make much improvement in their lives: they become victims of the sole process of learning how to remember things. They do not learn the technique of how to forget things. They only know how to learn; they do not know how to "unlearn." Because you do not know how to forget and unlearn, when you want to go to bed, to retire and relax your mind, you cannot really do this. You have not learned how to unlearn negative or disturbing things that you have learned. That creates serious problems all over the world, both in the West and the East, especially in the younger generation. Many things are constantly going on in your mind; your mind is thinking and thinking, and you cannot gain freedom from that process.

You suffer on account of many serious diseases that your mind creates, such as cancer, because you have not learned the method of unlearning, of how to be free when you want to be free. When you want to rest, you cannot; you are still thinking. That wall which stands between you and the Reality is your mind. All your training is applied to the mind, culturing and cultivating the mind. Books can tell you many things, but when you study your own mind, you may discover that today you are at peace, and feel that you have conquered your mind, but tomorrow you suddenly lose your temper. Perhaps you say something that is not to be said, or do something that should not be done. You constantly act like this, and you do not know from where in you this behavior is coming.

In human relationships, the most destructive of all weaknesses is the weakness of blaming others, as when you think, "I am suffering because of you," or, "I am unhappy because of you." You often blame others, just as you expect that others are going to make you happy. But no one has the capacity to make you happy. No one else has the capacity to make you blissful. Your mind is your own mind; it is your own samskaras that make you happy or unhappy.

To understand your samskaras, the impressions stored in the unconscious mind, you have to understand something about the mind/body relationship. If you glance at me, and then a few minutes later you look at me again, you will recognize me. This means that your optic nerve conducted an impression of me to your mind, where it was stored, and when you recall me again, this impression came forward.

Samskaras are the strong seeds that you have sown in various levels of your unconscious mind by your experiences and thoughts. They do not last for the duration of this lifetime alone. According to this teaching, if you believe in it, they lead to the next birth. They are not related only to this lifetime; they are very powerful motivations and affect the way you function, the way you think, feel, and even the things you desire. All these are due to your samskaras. Samskaras are the "seed memories" of your previous actions, which you have stored in the reservoir within yourself. Sometimes a time comes in your life when you feel helpless and at the mercy of your samskaras because you do not work with yourself, you do not sincerely do your practice, you do not improve yourself, and you do not really want to change your personality. That is why this feeling of helplessness occurs.

Let us first describe how samskaras affect you. The body is related to the mind. They are related to each other with the help of a force called *prana*, which is carried on the breath, the link between body and mind. As long as you are inhaling and exhaling, you live. When this process does not function, death occurs. The mind has two aspects, a conscious aspect and an unconscious aspect. The conscious part of the mind is only a small part of the totality of mind. It is the conscious aspect of mind that you have been training through your educational system. At the same time, you also pour into the unconscious mind all the experiences you have. When the experience we call "death" occurs, body, breath, and conscious mind fail, and they separate from the unconscious mind and from that higher unit called the Center of Consciousness.

Thus, down deep within you is a basement, in which you have stored all the seeds of your samskaras. The bubbles or impressions that disturb your behavior and your normal thinking process are still present there. Even if your wife, children, and friends tell you not to worry, you cannot stop it. No one wants you to worry, but you do it because of your learned habit patterns.

You can gain freedom from such a thinking process, which distorts and gives an entirely different sort of direction to your life, by understanding how to train yourself and then going in a different direction. However, you must really want to do this. That inner method of self-change is not taught in the external world. This internal method you will have to discover for yourself, by understanding a method called "journeying within." Journeying within tells you how to go inside.

Sometimes you think that nothing could be more powerful than what you consider "positive" in the external world. And yet even the object of your love has less power than your object of negativity. It is amazing to see how negativity controls your mind: you love those objects of negativity even more than the objects of love and positivity—that is why you think of them again and again. Something negative controls your life, and so the negative side of your life becomes more powerful than the positive side. You did not work with your own negative thought process, and now you are unhappy. However, you can gain

conscious control over yourself by making an effort—
using your human effort. A human being has the power to
make an effort: he can change his personality and utilize
the immense wealth, power, and brilliance buried within
himself. Once you learn to go to the inner chamber of your
being, you can do that. If you learn first how to decide to
change, and then how to determine within that you will not
repeat something negative, you can change yourself.

Perhaps you have a very bad temper; you get angry
and your anger is not controlled anger. You have not
learned to discipline yourself and this is very injurious to
you. You first have to analyze that anger: why do you get
so angry with someone that your speech is distorted and
you act very differently. At that time you feel different: you
forget yourself, your duties, and your relationships, and
you lose your temper and say things that are damaging and
injurious. If you analyze this process, you will find that in
the samskaras that you have deposited in the unconscious
mind, there are many desires that have not been fulfilled.
Perhaps you want to be respected by someone. If this
desire exists in you, it will hurt you so much that it will not
allow you to be at peace. You may think, "My partner
doesn't respect me." Then, you waste your time and energy
in such an expectation, with the hope that others will
respect you and love you. In this way, you become totally
dependent on others to fulfill your expectations. You do
nothing for yourself but expect things from others, which
is not a good thing to experience. But others have no
capacity to fulfill your expectations; these are *your* expectations. The mother of all problems and conflicts lies
within you, and that is expecting things from others.

Once, a journalist asked Mahatma Gandhi how to
attain happiness. Gandhi answered, "When you don't have
any desires, then you will be happy." Normally, you think,
"When I attain God, then I will be happy," but to be
practical, you have to recognize that when you don't have

any desires, it means that you have *fulfilled* all your desires, and then you are happy. But you should also develop a sense of discrimination and understanding about what desires are right or helpful for you to pursue. You should entertain only those desires that you can fulfill and that are right for you. If you have developed that capacity to discriminate between your desires, then you don't entertain those desires that are injurious to you and drive you crazy or create a state of helplessness. Unfulfilled desires within you will always lead to a state of unhappiness.

You should have some desires as a human being; you cannot live totally without desires. But those desires should be filtered by the sense of discrimination within you. Your buddhi, intelligence, has the function of judging, deciding, and discriminating which desires are useful. You should learn to develop that function within yourself. Then, decrease your desires. It is the useless desires that create problems for you, not appropriate or helpful desires. For example, the desire to eat food is not itself a problem, but sometimes you eat when you feel stress. When you experience stress, simply examine what that stress is, and consider whether you really need food or sleep or what you actually need. You may realize that your stress is the result of the thought that the person whom you love and who loves you does not respect you. Sometimes, such an intense desire to be respected and loved by others can create an obsession and a crazy state of mind. Expecting too much from others is always a problem. The happiest person is one who has very few expectations. You often question why you should help your partner or your friend if they don't help you. This sense of expectation, exchange, and bargaining leads you to a state of competition. When you think that way, you can never become creative and dynamic.

First, you need to understand yourself, and understanding yourself means knowing that while the body is subject to change, death, and decay, the soul is not. The soul is immortal. You need to understand your internal states, your mind, and its modifications. You need to observe how your buddhi functions, and how your manas (lower mind), ahamkara (ego), and chitta function. Chitta is the storehouse of knowledge and memories. Consider the reasons why others do not think the same way you think; you not only look different from others, but you think differently.

Deep down, you will find that the more selfish you are, the more you suffer in life. The one who suffers the most in life is he who is selfish, because he has not learned to let go; he has not learned to give. If you resist giving, then you won't ever enjoy life. You only make others suffer, and when you make others suffer, that tendency also leads you to self-suffering. Being selfish is actually hurting yourself; you want to deprive others of things and yet you want to be happy.

When you are selfish, you don't have consideration for others and you don't think of them. You think only about yourself—about your sensual joys, your superficial clinging, and your superficial desires. Those do not ever make you happy. During a time of selfishness, you feed someone called the ego. When you feed your ego, then for the sake of the ego you continually do many things without understanding the consequences. You may pray, but you are praying only to your ego. You are thinking, you are doing business, and you are talking to others according to the way your ego directs—you are behaving according to your ego's needs. Then, you do not improve and grow; you *cannot* improve because you are only feeding your ego. The ego is that which has separated you from the whole, and that is why you are miserable. The law of expansion is not being expressed when you are selfish, and instead you are fulfilling only the law of contraction.

When you learn to work with yourself gently and gradually, you can change your personality. You can change your whole being if you really want to, because you can change your masks. Those masks that you wear have been chosen and made by you, but you can change them and make your personality a pleasant one. Work with your samskaras: if you make a sincere human effort, you will learn that all your actions do, indeed, give you their fruits. There is no such thing as an action that does not give a fruit. This is a scientific law: every action has its reaction. No one can overturn this law. When you make a sincere human effort, you sometimes feel that you are not improving, but that is not possible. If you do not see progress, then it may be that you are not making an effort truthfully, with full determination, and with all your might. The moment you start to do that, you will find that there is a dynamic change in your thinking, behavior, and in your writing. Do an experiment in this manner for even just a day or two: use that great power that is your inherent power—the power called love. Learn to express yourself in such a way that you don't hurt, injure, or harm others.

Yoga science explains profoundly the true meaning of love. In the set of personal commitments that you make, the *yamas* and *niyamas,* yoga science advises you to practice ahimsa. Ahimsa means non-injuring, non-harming or non-violence. To practice ahimsa means not to harm, hurt or injure those with whom you live. Often you hurt others merely for the sake of your own selfish ego. If you learn to practice ahimsa, then you are practicing love. To practice ahimsa means practicing love in your daily life, and the practice of love does not mean being selfish. Consider how many times a day you have a desire to give the wealth and bounty you have to others, even to those with whom you are related. The ability to give to outsiders develops later on. Ahimsa should be practiced first, with those close to you and truth is practiced later; truth will follow by itself.

When you have learned to enjoy giving, a time will come when you can give without any reservation. Giving the fruits of your actions to others, whether known or unknown to you, is a different process. But, first, you have to learn to give at home or wherever you live—with your friends, your relatives, and those to whom you are closely related—your wife, husband, and children. Do not give up and tell yourself that this is just the way you are, and that you cannot change.

If you accept the idea that you cannot change, then you cannot do anything in life. You will be a total failure: then, you cannot be creative and you cannot improve. If this is how you live, then what is the use of living? Such a life is boring and becomes a burden to you. You should continue to do experiments with yourself, and every time you do one, you will find that you are growing and growing. Your growth should lead you to such a state and a height in which you are free from all desires that are selfish. The desires to help others, to serve others, and to serve the nation or humanity—these are great desires. When all your small desires are swallowed by that great desire, then your life will be like that of a saint. You will find yourself to have become entirely different. All the truly great men and women who have lived on this earth have been totally selfless and desireless; they lived for the sake of others, to serve and help others. They knew the cosmic principle—that the only way to freedom is to learn to give. This is the law of life: give and give up.

If you study yourself, you can consider why and for whom your hands and feet work—they work to feed your mouth. If your hands and feet decide to no longer feed the mouth, you will not survive. Your teeth grind and chew your food for your liver, and your liver functions for the whole being. In fact, your whole being lives for the entire universe—this is a fact.

You are acting against this principle when you work only for yourself. You are becoming selfish, and this process is one of degeneration; that is why you suffer. The

main cause of your suffering is your selfishness and egotism. Being selfish means that you are not doing your
duties, and if you are not doing your duties, you cannot
expect to experience happiness. Being egotistical means
you are going downhill; you are not progressing or
improving.

In all the great cultures of the world there have been
great men who are examples for you. If you study their
lives you will learn that they were sometimes crucified,
killed, rebuked, or stoned to death for the sake of others,
not for themselves. Petty men die for themselves and for
their own petty desires, but great men die because they
want to serve humanity. Both kinds of people die, but there
is a difference in both their dying and their living.

A good person really *lives.* How can a person who is
not healthy or helpful for himself be healthy and helpful to
others? Such a person who suffers from himself cannot
love others, and cannot perform actions that are selfless.
Such a person creates a whirlpool for himself; he cannot
cross the mire of delusion that arises in his own mind or go
beyond. He cannot rise. Do not give up on yourself by
deciding that you cannot do it, that you cannot improve.
You sometimes conclude that you are a bad person and
condemn yourself. Does thinking of yourself as bad mean
that you have a bad face, or clothes, or a bad home, or bad
parents? What do such negative thoughts mean? You
constantly identify yourself with your negative habit patterns, and that is why you think of yourself as bad or weak.

Your negative thoughts often involve going back into
the past; you remember the events of the past and then you
think of yourself as bad. You identify yourself with your
past actions. If you allow yourself to go on thinking in that
way, you will never improve. You will never come out of
the past, and then you will never enjoy either the present or
the future. You have to emerge from dwelling on the past,
since that makes you think that you are bad or small or

petty or good-for-nothing. You have to decide that you are neither bad, weak nor limited. Perhaps, for example, a woman was divorced by her husband because he was a selfish man. The woman may decide, "I must be so unlovable that he can't love me, and that's why he has divorced me." But actually, the man divorced her because he has a bad habit. The divorce is the result of his problem, not hers, but if she assumes those problems as her own, then she suffers.

The sense of identification with the negative has always been a human weakness. You identify yourself with negative emotions, thoughts, and traits. Perhaps you have done some negative things in your life. Then decide that you will not continue to do such things anymore. You make an effort and decide not to continue to do those actions. You originally did those actions against your own conscience, and you knew that you should not have done them, but you did, even though it was against your own personal philosophy. During your life, you do many such things, and then you identify yourself with those actions and form a new, negative personality.

Then, you decide that you are a bad person. You decide that you are weak and cannot do anything. You wonder if it is possible for you to be enlightened or to attain a state that is free from all your problems, emotions, pains, and miseries. You feel unhappy and helpless and that is why you cannot meditate—because you do not have confidence. You may sit and close your eyes and try to meditate. You want to meditate, but suddenly your mind tells you that you are bad, or condemns you or makes you feel worthless, and then you cannot meditate.

The moment you decide that you are not going to repeat actions that are unhealthy for you or your growth, then you are free. All your prayers help you to achieve that. You pray to God to give you strength, but your strength has been diminished by your actions—by actions

that are not in accordance with your ethics or your own
conscience. Any action that you think is bad for you is also
bad for others. With this feeling, you walk the earth,
constantly depressed and disappointed in life. You should
learn to help yourself—every human being is a somewhat
sick person, and the sick are creating more sick. You need
to learn to help yourself and you have the capacity to do
that. You can help yourself by beginning the journey called
the "inward journey," through which you come to understand yourself and the various levels of your life by studying each level, one after another.

One of your major problems is that you do not fully
know, understand, and accept yourself. Thus, you remain
dependent on the suggestions and support of others.

In fact, most of your problems and ailments are created
for you by those who claim to love you. They give you a
sickness, and you call it love. What you call love is a
sickness, because you become dependent on that person
and his or her support and suggestions, and then you
expect too much from that particular person or object. The
weakness is really yours—it is not the object of love that
disappoints you; it is your own expectations that disappoint you. The more you expect from others, the more
you are disappointed. Your expectations are beyond all
limits, while every object of the world has some limit. That
disparity makes you suffer. If you really want to remain
healthy, sleep well, and avoid disturbing your rest with
strange dreams or nightmares, then do not allow yourself
to uselessly and unrealistically expect things. Your exces-
sive and useless expectations are very harmful and injurious to you.

You can go to a therapist, and the therapist may
explore your problem and tell you the reason for your
unhappiness. But if you have a habit, then you will create
that misery for yourself again and again. You need to learn
to be free from your own habit patterns. Presently, your

mind travels in particular grooves that you have created for yourself. Your mind refuses to come out of those grooves and simply repeats certain thoughts. The real experts—the sages and teachers—say that to change, you have to create new grooves in your mind, so that the mind travels, instead, in those new grooves. When the mind starts traveling in new grooves, then your habit patterns will change, because your thoughts will change and then your personality will also change.

History tells us that even the worst man can become a sage. Remember that this is what happened to both St. Paul and the Indian sage Valmiki. Whether you look at the Sufi tradition, Chinese history or Japanese history, you will find that in all of them, great people have transformed themselves. You will find great human beings, and learn that although those human beings were not initially good or wise—in fact, they may even have been the worst people—they were able to change their entire characters and personalities. Even murderers and habitual criminals have changed their personalities. You are not any worse than Saul. If Saul could become St. Paul, then you can also transform yourself. History tells you that you have the power, capacity, and ability to change yourself, provided you decide to do it! When you have learned how to decide, how to make a resolution, when you work to increase your determination, then you can change your personality. You can become a great sage like Saul. That is the path of changing the heart.

The difference between an ordinary man and a sage is that a sage is strong from within and does not allow anyone to affect his mind and emotions. The Buddha demonstrated this in the village of Rajgrahi when he left his throne, renounced his kingdom, and went to that small village to perform austerities. He went to beg for alms. Begging helps one to reduce the ego. He was a prince, but he wanted to be the world's simplest man. At that time, there were thousands of monks in Rajgrahi, which was a small village. Almost every third person was a monk and it became impossible for the people to feed them all.

So one day the Buddha went out begging with Ananda, his main disciple, who used to accompany him. They had a particular saying, "Narayana, Hari," which means, "Remember God's name." When people hear that, they know that someone has come to the door for *bhiksha*. The Buddha was a quiet man, and he stood outside, but when he arrived at one house, the mother became very angry.

"You are a healthy man, a strong man, a handsome man, standing at our door—and I don't have that much food to give. I have already given away food to many other monks. What shall I give you? I'm only a poor lady. Go away! Don't you have any other place to go?!"

The Buddha merely smiled gently. Then she said, "Wait, I will give you bhiksha," and she picked up the filth from her child, the stool, and wanted to give it to the Buddha, saying, "This is what you deserve!"

But the Buddha merely smiled and said simply, "Mother, you can keep it. I don't need it."

Then Ananda was very angry and said, "Woman, you are insulting my lord and master; I'll kill you!"

But the Buddha said to Ananda, "Stop! She wants to give me something, but if I don't need it, I don't take it, so why are you angry?"

This is the important question: when people try to give you their anger or negative feedback, why do you accept it? If someone says that you are bad, why do you accept that? You accept it because you do not have self-confidence; you do not accept yourself and know deep inside that you are good. You do not really know yourself, and you have formed the habit of living in dependence on others' judgments. In your heart of hearts, you should never accept negative suggestions from those who are near you; this can create a very serious problem for you.

You have not been taught to have confidence in yourself. Your present sense of confidence means only that ten other people have told you you look beautiful, so you become dependent on their support. If you tell someone that they are beautiful, they reply, "You made my day." Thus, when others tell you that you are beautiful, you accept it, but you do not realize it before. You expect others to constantly give you such compliments, and then you become dependent on them.

Because you are dependent and insecure, you constantly create ego problems with others. A few years ago, I decided to study the question of divorce. I wanted to know where the problem was, and I discovered that the problem of divorce actually originates with your ego. One such divorce was very interesting to consider: this husband and wife were well-known actors in Chicago, and unfortunately, they came for my blessings before they got married. I was happy for them and I prayed, "Dear God, make them happy." But if you make yourself unhappy, then what can God do? It didn't work: after a week they fought about their tube of toothpaste. There was a serious ego conflict about this petty matter and so they divorced! This is an ego problem: you are not prepared to learn from others, and you are not prepared to understand others. Yet you still say that you love each other!

Your ego is the representative of Atman in the individual self, but it has forgotten itself and its real duty; the ego has become external. Actually the ego is a very important function, but, if you do not know how to use, train, and "polish" the ego, it is a serious barrier to your growth. If your ego is properly understood and trained, then it can be a great help. The ego is a great force; it is the main modification of your mind. But your ego should not become a barrier to the development of your love.

Often your love does not grow and develop because your love does not grow from a state of understanding.

Love means first understanding each other, and then accepting each other as you are. Many husbands become great "teachers" for their wives; all the time they try to teach her or tell her what to do. This is an ego problem; the wife never married her husband so that he could become her teacher. She never expected that, and is upset. Many wives also assert their power with their husbands, "You should do this because you are my husband. Unfortunately, I married you. Now, you should do what I want." Then a tussle comes and no one wins.

Married people often talk about this; let the married women or men sit down together, and they will talk about how much they control their spouses. Observe how you injure each other so much in the name of love! This happens because that bridge of mutual understanding is not being built by people. A relationship becomes very easy if you understand each other and accept each other as you are—then you can help each other. There are always shortcomings in every human life, and you realize those shortcomings in each other after you get married, but not before that, when you are boyfriend and girlfriend. You have to learn to accept each other and not love only the superficial. Your attraction to these superficial attractions robs the chastity of your love's beauty, and then you don't appreciate others' inner beauty or their good qualities.

In life, there are two processes going on simultaneously—accepting and rejecting things. When I walk, I am rejecting the old space and accepting a new space. When you swim, you push the water away in order to go forward. You also do that when you exhale. You reject carbon dioxide and accept fresh air. Learn not to accept negative feedback or the idea that you are a bad person. You hear what others say and then you go home and feel sad; you really accept their suggestions and you start to conclude, "Really, I must be bad. I am not good enough. They say I am bad, so I must be." This kind of acceptance of others' suggestions can even lead a person to need psychiatric treatment eventually, if that person is weak.

Observe your own thinking processes and your internal states, but don't accept such negative suggestions from any quarter. Certainly, you commit mistakes, and you should learn to rectify those mistakes. You become free by not repeating a mistake; do not brood over it. The power of prayer is that you pour out all your superficial tendencies of mind—your faults and desires—and instead, you try to be in touch with the deepest and finest level of your being, the Center of Consciousness within, from where Consciousness flows on various degrees and grades. You say, "O Lord, I want Shakti; I want power, I want the energy to handle this situation." And you can do it, if you have learned to practice and to rely upon your internal resources.

External resources do help you to accomplish external things, but only internal sources really help you and make you strong. This is very important: there are two different sorts of resources—the external, superficial, momentary, and transitory external resources, and the real internal resources, which are permanent and unchanging. You should understand that you are fully equipped with all the resources and power that you need, but usually, you do not tap that; you have formed a habit of seeking help in the external world. Such reliance is not safe; it's merely a crutch. The more you rely on yourself and learn from your mistakes, then the stronger you become. If you commit a mistake, then learn from it. Great people learn through their mistakes. To commit a mistake is human, but to go on committing mistakes is a sin. Once you know something is injurious for you, you can decide not to continue to commit that mistake because it does not allow you to grow, it does not change your personality or make you happy.

Your personality can be changed. In this lifetime, you can attain the highest rung of life, a state free from pain and misery. Don't postpone this, as you postpone the other joys of your life. Enlightenment is your birthright; that state is freedom from pain and misery. Enlightenment is not something acquired or new—it is already there. You can realize that state. Learn to work with yourself to remove the barriers to your growth. Learn to transform your habits and, thus, purify and perfect your personality. This is your challenge—to transform your own personality!

Chapter 4

The Nature
of Negative Emotions

If I move my hand and make certain gestures as I speak, what prompts me to do that? Most of our gestures are actually unconscious. So perhaps as I speak, my fingers are moving or some other part of my body is moving. The body has a particular language of its own, which we call "body language." The body creates such gestures and movements because all its actions are governed and controlled by the thoughts. Any movement means that some thought that exists in the mind is being expressed. This is an important point: your actions are controlled by, and are the result of, your thoughts, both conscious and unconscious.

The branch of knowledge that deals with your thinking and feeling life is called "psychology" in the modern time. You should understand your mind and its modifications on deeper levels by observing and analyzing your body language and behavior, and then seek to understand why your body moves or reacts in a particular way.

Everything your body does has a meaning: if you overeat, you burp. If your body aches or is stiff, you will move in a certain way. When your body is in pain, others can tell from your movements that there is something wrong with you and that you are in pain. Your gestures are totally influenced by your thought processes.

Actually, the English word "man" is related to the Sanskrit word, *mana,* which means "mind," so to fully know and understand yourself as a human being, you must first understand your own mind, by studying yourself.

However, you cannot really know your mind in its totality, for a vast part of the mind remains buried and unknown to you, and is never understood. In discussing the nature of mind, we often say, "All of the body is in the mind, but all of the mind is *not* in the body." This means that the mind itself is actually much more vast and expansive than the mere physical body. Thus, if you want to fully understand your mind, you will have to eliminate your negative assumption that you are only a small and limited creature and that's your extent or limit. You usually only think of yourself in limited terms; for example, you think that you are too weak or too thin or too fat or too short. You cannot imagine that someone like you could have a great and powerful mind. You habitually identify yourself with your limitations and weaknesses, not with your highest nature.

But this understanding of yourself is not accurate: within you lies something great and powerful—the mind. It can certainly become a wall or barrier between you and the Reality, but at the same time, it can also become a means that you can use to help you attain the highest goal in life—to know that dimension of life that is presently unknown to you. You can understand that part of your personality of which you are presently unaware, by understanding the various functions of your mind and its totality.

In your religious education, you were taught that Jesus Christ was a great man; he was the Son of God. According to the Vedantic analysis, this is true. Moses, too, was a son of God, as were Buddha, Krishna, Mohammed, and Guru

Nanak. They were all born on the earth in exactly the same way that you were born. When Jesus wanted to see, he used his eyes; when he wanted to hear, he used his ears. He walked on the earth exactly like you, so why is he considered to be such a great leader? He was truly great and powerful because he knew the inner dimensions of life and the laws that motivate them to function. He knew his internal states; he knew his own mind.

Like all the great ones, in order to make spiritual progress, you first need to understand your own thinking process, and actually there are many levels to understand in your thinking process.

A writer once beautifully said, "If a good thought is not brought into action, it's either a kind of treachery or an abortion." This means that that which is good within you should be expressed. But what is a "good thought"? A good thought is that which makes you creative, a thought that does not create conflicts within you—that is a good thought. A good thought is that which makes you peaceful, tranquil, balanced, happy, and joyous. Such a thought should not be allowed to die unexpressed within yourself, nor should it remain asleep or dormant within. It should be expressed through your mind, action, and speech.

So as far as observing your thoughts is concerned, you need to learn to select or reject from among your many thoughts. Learn to reject those thoughts that are disturbing to you. But there is a problem or difficulty in doing this: you know what is right and wrong or good and bad for yourself. You know this and even animals know it, so why do you do things that should not be done, and lack the motivation to do those things which you should do? The simple answer is, that this is due to your habits. Habits are a very strong force in the human mind and personality, but unfortunately, you do not appreciate their power. There is an important question you need to understand: how are your negative habits formed?

Consider who you are: you have a personality, and your personality is controlled by your particular and unique character. Over the course of your life and growth, your character has been woven by your habit patterns. You have a particular habit, and your spouse has a different type of habit, and thus, you decide that you are not compatible, yet you are both good people. Your habit patterns feed your individual egos, and then you create a division or barrier between yourself and others, and you remain inside that ego boundary. The same thing happens to your spouse. You are both wonderful people, but you are not compatible because your habit patterns are different and conflicting.

Your habit patterns weave a mask for you, and that becomes what and who you are. You call it your personality, but who are you really? You are the way you have made yourself—that is what and who you are. You have manufactured something for yourself to wear, and that is a mask—your personality. Sometimes the mask exists for defense or protection, sometimes the mask exists to deflect others, sometimes it is for creative purposes. You use this mask of the personality for many purposes.

But in reality, you dismiss the fact that your personality is what you have made yourself, and then you say, "This is just the way I am!" or, "God has made me the way I am," which means that you also do not understand the word, "God." The word, "God," stands for that principle of equality, love, and selfless brilliance—the *summum bonum* of life. You should not misuse the idea of God to claim that God created you the way you are. You are a spark of the Great Light, there is no doubt about that. That Great Light which is within you is actually a nucleus, and this whole universe is its expansion. You'll understand this truth only when you have realized the Truth. But you constantly identify yourself with your body, your thoughts, and with the objects of the world.

The main cause of your suffering is your own pattern of identifying yourself with the objects of the world and with your thinking patterns. You think, "I am bad; I am good for nothing. I cannot do anything," and then you become negative. You want to be loved all the time, and it is true that love is the Lord of life. But observe what happens inside you if you hate one person and you love someone else. Notice the process: your hatred is intense for the one whom you dislike, but your love for the other is not of such intensity. So, unfortunately, in human life, your hatred goes to deeper levels within you than your love, because you are not careful about how your emotions are deepened and intensified. You repeat and intensify negative emotions until they become a powerful habit.

But if you remain careful with your emotions, and learn how to go through the ups and downs of life and still remain balanced, then you will not suffer from the many diseases that plague you. Some of the diseases that you experience are the result of negative emotions that you do not yet recognize, nor are their causes understood even by medical science.

You have everything that you need around you; there is someone to tell you, "Honey, I love you." Your child says, "Mom, I love you." You have a beautiful home, and yet you are not at peace. This is not due to your thinking patterns alone, because actually, there is something even deeper than thoughts. Beneath your thinking process lies the power of emotion. In your daily life among your friends and families, both at home and at work, you sometimes realize, or others tell you that you're an emotional wreck. You realize that you've become too emotional and are not emotionally balanced. When this happens, it is because you have not properly understood or organized your emotional life.

To begin to work with the conflicts and emotions within, you first need to better understand the nature of emotions themselves. You should realize that emotion is one of the greatest powers that you have within you. Human emotion is a very powerful force, but everything depends upon how you use that force in your life, for such power can either be expressed very creatively or very destructively.

The sages who learned to tap that power made it creative, like Chaitanya Mahaprabhu in India. He came into contact with that emotional power directly, and he channelled it through a kind of chanting. Chanting is totally unlike crying, which is another way people express emotions. When you cry, you experience pain and misery, but when you chant, you are in joy. Using your emotions in a r~gative way involves doing things like crying and being miserable. Using your emotion in a creative way means chanting, singing, making poems, and dancing—but actually, it's the same emotional power!

The Book of Wisdom—the Upanishads—the most ancient of the scriptures in the library of man, says, "O man, if you truly understand that power within you, then you know you are God yourself. If you do not yet understand who you really are, then you are still a brute, and when you understand who you are a little bit, then you are a human being."

You each have all three of these qualities within you: the divine, the human, and the animal. When you experience your animal emotions, then you suddenly forget your children, your husband or wife, and your friends. You become wild and forget your responsibilities and relationships. And when you forget your responsibilities, it means that you are not in touch with your internal states, which exist on many dimensions.

Emotion plays a powerful role in life. When you are upset, disorganized, or emotionally out of control, you say things that you don't really mean. Later, you're sorry, but what prompted you to say that negative thing in the first place? You need to understand what prompted you to become wild and to have that emotional outburst. You never really meant to hurt anybody, so then you apologize to those you love, "I'm sorry, I didn't mean to hurt you. I love you, and I'm sorry I said that," but the next day you repeat the same behavior, because you do not understand your own emotions and from where your behavior arises.

This does not mean that you are a bad person, or have ugliness inside you, but it means that you have not yet learned to organize, direct, and lead that great emotional power. Someone who knows how to lead and direct his or her emotional power can attain in a short time, the same height of ecstasy as that achieved by a yogi who does intense practices for many years to attain samadhi. Both processes are the same, provided you know how to channel your emotions and have learned how to go beyond the mire of delusion created by your own mind and its thinking process. This is possible when you understand the origins of your emotions.

Emotions can be powerful in either positive and negative ways. Perhaps, for example, you are driving your car and you suddenly see that a small puppy is caught in a bush and is crying helplessly. The puppy does not belong to you, but if you are in touch with your creative emotions at that time, you may stop and try to help the puppy. Such emotions can lead you to creativity and positive action, but there are also negative emotions, which can lead you to disaster and can destroy your life.

It is important to understand the negative emotions, to know what they are, and from where they arise. The spiritual scriptures of the ancients that describe the path of sadhana have analyzed the negative emotions and categorized them. The first of all these emotions is kama, the prime desire. Kama is the mother of all other desires, and it gives rise to both the desire to satisfy or gratify the senses, and the beneficial desire to help others selflessly. Kama is the prime desire, and from it arise all the other desires.

If kama is not fulfilled, then you become frustrated and angry (*krodha*). When you become angry, it actually means that one of your desires is unfulfilled, and that prompts you to become angry. The complete and accurate definition of anger is the emotion resulting from unfulfilled desires that you have not learned how to arrange, to pacify, or to understand. Thus, anger means that there is some desire that needs to be understood and resolved.

If your desire is achieved and kama is fulfilled, then pride, or *muda* results. Thus, when the desire is fulfilled, you become proud, but if it is not fulfilled, then you become angry. Because of this, you need to be careful to observe yourself clearly. When a desire is fulfilled, you should observe whether it feeds your pride, and if it is not fulfilled, observe whether it feeds your anger. You have to watch yourself carefully for these two reactions. You need to learn to make inner experiments with your own emotions when you seek to work with yourself and go within. This subject of how to work with your own emotions and develop yourself fully is usually never taught or discussed in daily life.

In fact, to the serious student, there is only one real book to study and learn from—the greatest of all books—and that is the very manuscript that you, yourself, are. This manuscript has been written by you; you are the author of your life. If you want to learn, this is the book from which you must study!

Now comes the next step in the analysis: when a desire is fulfilled and you attain what you long for, then you become attached to it. This attachment is called *moha*, the sense "This is mine!" Once you attain something, you become attached and you want to keep it, repeat the experience, and fear losing it.

Actually, there is an irony in life: when you say, "This is mine," the object actually is not yours, and on the other hand, when you claim, "This is not mine," then actually it *is* yours. You'll constantly observe in life that you claim that something is yours or that something else is not yours. What an ineffable condition! This body is yours, for example, but you have no control over it. You make such false claims your whole life. You live with these false claims; sometimes you laugh about them and sometimes you cry. Sometimes you become overwhelmed with pride for all your achievements or accomplishments. Sometimes you become disturbed emotionally because certain important desires of your desire-world have not been fulfilled.

Then comes the next step, *lobha:* when you are attached to something, you become greedy. This greed is never fulfilled, no matter what you do. Once you are attached to something, you can never have enough! The fire of greed is horrible! The fire of your greed is so intense that you cannot believe its destructiveness—it can even make you sick. There are actually diseases in which greed and longing lead to physical illness. Such an emotion can make you obsessed with something. Then, when you become greedy, you also become jealous of others and insecure by comparing yourself to them.

Once, I visited a Greek Orthodox Church in the midwest with one of my students who is a doctor. Next to us we noticed a woman who was wearing a huge diamond and expensive clothes, but she was frowning and gesturing all the time and talking out loud, and she disrupted the entire service. She kept watching others and talking out loud: "What does she think of herself? I have a better diamond than she does. I have a more beautiful dress." She was a very rich woman, but she was obsessively jealous of her neighbor, so whatever she did, she did it only to show off for the neighbor, and this became an emotional sickness.

Whatever you do—whether it is the kind of clothes you wear, the way you walk or the way you talk—do not do it for others. If your neighbor does something, so you also do it, it makes you become a kind of "reactionary." Something destructive happens to you: you lose touch with yourself and you become a mere reactor to others. Then, you don't do what you really value, think or believe; you do only what others value. When this happens you no longer live for yourself; you begin to live for others in a very negative way. Often, you live for your neighbors in such a negative fashion. Perhaps your neighbors dislike you, so you dislike the neighbors, and that's how you live your whole life. Then, hatred and jealousy become a part of your life.

You constantly compare yourself with others. What is that thing called "beauty" that you feel so insecure and worry so much about? You are the only one, a unique entity created by Providence. There is no duplication or repetition in the world, so if everything is unique, then who is beautiful and who is ugly? Everything is beautiful! To think that something is beautiful and something different is ugly is a superimposition on reality that occurs only in your thinking. You judge that one thing is good and another is bad, but such concepts are impositions by your mind, by your thinking, and by your impoverished philosophy of life.

When I first visited the United States, the third or fourth day that I was here, I told somebody, "You are beautiful," and she replied, "Oh, you just made my day!" You often react to other's praise this way. Your reaction means that you are constantly craving and needing another's appreciation. For example, a wife looks to her husband for appreciation, and if he says a kind word to her—"Oh, you are so beautiful!" then the wife hugs and kisses him. But this dependence on others' support or praise is not dealing with reality; it is merely living on the strength of others' approval and appreciation, and then you develop weak and unreal ways of thinking.

What is this process of life? We live on certain levels;

we have created certain values for ourselves, and that's how we live. Then, we think *that* is Reality, and yes, it's real, because reality is a relative term, but the waking reality is different than the dreaming reality, and the dream reality is different than the sleeping reality, but the Absolute Reality lies beyond. He who knows only how to live in this waking reality, adjusting and reacting to everyone, is a fool.

Perhaps you cannot deal with certain problems or conflicts at home, and so you go to study with a swami or a yogi, or you start doing japa. Avoiding the emotional issue is not going to help you. Often, instead of dealing with the conflict or issue, you look for answers outside yourself, and of course, you don't succeed. Learn, instead, to understand the origins of your emotions, the places from where these emotions spring.

The next and sixth major stream of emotion is ahamkara, the sense of "I-am-ness." This little "I," which you use every day to refer to yourself and not to others, becomes the center of your life. That word that you use again and again in your daily life, "I," becomes the center of your awareness. You say, "I am doing this; I am not doing that; I do not want to do this." All this is the work of ahamkara. You have created a fortress; you have created a barrier with your own ego, and then you do not know how to come out of it in order to know the highest Reality. You use all your differences, your defense mechanisms, to protect yourself and your ahamkara.

You need to understand what ahamkara does for you: the sense of I-ness prompts you to live on the earth, and to have a particular individuality. Because of ahamkara, you are an individual, but then ahamkara also separates you from the whole. When a wife and husband, two lovers, touch a peak that is beyond ahamkara, that is real joy. Ahamkara itself will never give you joy; instead, it will contract your personality. It enables you to be an individual, but it will never give you joy.

You only attain joy when you completely forget ahamkara, when you are no longer limited by ahamkara. But how is it possible for you to live without a sense of I-ness? That's not possible, so it is better to "polish" your ahamkara. Just as you polish your shoes and use them every day, and then, eventually, they are worn out, so should you polish your ahamkara—your ego.

All your prayers, all your loves, all your concerns, all your friendships, anything that you consider important in your life, you do because of ahamkara. You think that you love your husband and he thinks that he loves you, but really you each love your own ahamkara. That's why you love others.

There is a beautiful saying in Sanskrit, which is translated, "Why do you love your wife, your children and others? For yourself; for if you yourself did not exist, how could you love anybody?" If you love others for the sake of their Atman, pure Consciousness, that is very good, but usually, you only love them for the sake of your ahamkara.

In most of what you do, you do not do the action for the sake of the action alone, and you do not genuinely love someone, or pray to God, or do any good thing—instead it is the expression of your ahamkara. A rich man's ahamkara is to give donations and to feel proud of his generosity. The rich man doesn't really want to give even a penny; he is greedy, but he wants even more to satisfy his ahamkara. You all want to satisfy your ahamkara. Ahamkara is the great fortress that you have created for yourself; it locks you in and others out—but you can polish your ego and use the ahamkara up.

Thus, there are six main streams of emotions. Two are primary: kama and ahamkara. Kama is the prime desire, and ahamkara is the sense of "I", that which makes you think, "I am this. This is mine. This is not mine. This is mine and that is yours." That is what ahamkara does. Now, you should understand the origin of ahamkara. How have you become like this? Is this the way you are created by God? We will explore the root of this question and this philosophy so that you understand it more fully.

If you consider who you are and your deepest nature, you can compare yourself to a wheel. A wheel cannot rotate if it lacks spokes; the spokes allow the wheel to rotate, but the spokes will not rotate if there is no hub. The hub of the wheel is the part that remains still and does not move. The entire wheel rotates because of the hub, which does not rotate. That central something which does not itself move, somehow allows the entire wheel to move—it creates movement.

Such is the case with human beings: there is something called the individual soul or the Center of Consciousness, which is not subject to movement, change, destruction or death. Like the hub of a wheel, it does not move. That central part of us is eternal, but we are not in touch with this center, and so we are constantly afraid and insecure. We become caught up by our emotions. We hardly ever come into contact with that part of our being that is the Center of Consciousness. From this Center of Consciousness, consciousness flows on various degrees and grades. That little bit of consciousness that we presently experience is only a dim consciousness.

If you place a light inside of many levels of shades or filters, one after another, the light seen outside will be very dim. But if you take away all the shades, one by one, the light will get brighter as you remove each one. This Light is your Reality. You are like the unmoving hub within the wheel or the light inside the shades, but you do not identify yourself with the Center; you identify yourself with the spokes, with those lower aspects that move and change!

If we continue the metaphor of the wheel, you need to understand that there are four main spokes to your wheel. One is manas, which you call "mind." You don't really understand anything about what the mind is. Manas is merely one aspect of your thinking process. It raises questions, such as, "Shall I do this or not?" Whenever you consider doing something, suddenly a questioning comes into your mind, and you wonder, "Shall I do it or not? Shall I go this way or that way? Which is more useful? Shall I sit here or there? Shall I speak to you or not?" There is always a doubtful nature to your mind, and that is the result of the faculty of manas. This constant doubt in your mind is *sankalpa vikalpa.* There is only one power in you that works both within and outside, and this is manas. Manas can work inside, and it can also work outside yourself. To do that, it employs the ten senses. Manas begins to work the moment you wake up: You think, "Oh, I should have a cup of tea," so your hand moves, you walk toward the kitchen, and you start to make tea.

Manas itself, however, is limited and has no power to make decisions. The faculty that decides is buddhi, the faculty of discrimination. Buddhi has three aspects: the first is the power to discriminate between things: this is a man and this is a woman, or this is good and this is bad— that's discrimination. The second power is the power to decide, and the third is the power to judge. Thus, the main qualities of buddhi are the powers of discrimination, judgment, and decision.

There is a third faculty of mind called chitta, the reservoir of knowledge and memory, of merits and demerits. Chitta contains the power of becoming from inside, and also the accumulation of knowledge from outside.

There is also a fourth faculty, ahamkara, or the sense of I-ness, which we have described earlier. Thus, in this wheel of life, there are four main spokes that rotate the wheel. You should learn to distinguish between them and understand their nature and how they affect you. Finally, and even more importantly, there is also the hub, the silent witness, the Center of Consciousness.

The lower faculties of mind include two trouble makers:

manas and ahamkara. When you want to do something, you worry and doubt and say, "Shall I do it or not?" Thus, your manas disturbs you with doubts and questions, but if you calm down and ask the faculty of buddhi, you'll come to the right judgement. You all have these two qualities. One way of working with yourself and with these two qualities is self-counseling.

How do you begin to counsel yourself? You cannot see an external counselor or therapist every day to solve your problems. First, you should learn to observe and understand something about yourself. One important question is, "Is my first thought good or bad—is it clear or clouded?" Sometimes your initial thought is very helpful and if you follow it, you are successful. Sometimes if you think twice, and then do what your second thought suggests, that is better. You need to learn for yourself, is your first thought a guiding thought or not? Does your second thought guide you more clearly, and does your third thought lead you to confusion or to clarity? This is something you should learn about yourself by observing how your mind operates while self-counseling—to know when you should trust the advice of your mind. When you learn that, it is extremely helpful to you.

Sometimes you should doubt your own doubts. Perhaps you have a doubt about whether someone else is good or bad, so you look outside yourself and start analyzing that other person. Instead, examine your own thoughts and ask yourself to doubt your own doubts. Then the whole problem will vanish: the other person is a good person. Just as you can look at others with negativity, you can also see another's positive qualities. At present, you are in doubt and you see both their negative and positive qualities. Which kind of perception and mental attitude do you want to promote in yourself? You have three personalities: the divine in you, which is a symbol of love; the human in you, and the animal in you. Which do you want to promote?

Your education, environment, and family circumstances all contribute to your emotional development.
Knowing the purpose of life contributes much to your
happiness. You need to learn what else you can do to be
happy and emotionally balanced. Self-counseling is a very
interesting subject, and it is actually a dialogue within
yourself. If such self-counseling is done systematically and
consciously, then it is a wonderful and very powerful
process. You all think that you need therapists, but you
can learn to counsel yourself. This is the real aim of
spiritual teachers. Teachers who know how to counsel
within can, first, help themselves, and thus, by helping
themselves, they can also help others.

If you train manas, and if you lead your ahamkara
toward chitta and your manas toward buddhi, then you
have accomplished something. Don't do anything in life
unless your buddhi, the counselor within, tells you to do it.
You need to make internal experiments with yourself: you
need to train your buddhi to give a correct, clear judgment
to your manas. You also have to train your manas to take
the advice of buddhi. The nature of buddhi is clear and it is
very useful, but sometimes you don't want to listen to your
own buddhi. Perhaps you feel deprived of something of
value, and suddenly the idea occurs that you want to steal
it. You know that it's wrong, yet you want to do it. This is
due to your mental habits. So you must train both your
manas and your ahamkara, and that process is what we
call polishing your ahamkara.

Now, let us come back to the subject of how the
negative emotions arise. As we said, there are six main
streams of emotion: the prime desire *(kama)*, anger *(krodha)*,
pride *(muda)*, attachment *(moha)*, greed *(lobha)*, and I-
ness *(ahamkara)*. From where do these six streams come?
They must flow from someplace, since they're not the
result of your Divine nature. This is a very important
subject. The origin of these streams is in the four primitive

fountains. If you learn this lesson well, it will help you in all areas of life.

What are those primitive fountains? They are food, sex, sleep, and self-preservation. All human beings and all creatures have these urges. There's not a very big difference between human beings and animals in these urges. In fact, seat your dog in front of you and you will find that in some ways you are inferior. If the dog was trained not to eat a dog biscuit, it leaves the biscuit there, but you don't have such self-control: any time you want to, you eat!

These four primitive fountains are the real source of all emotions. If you eat unhealthy or bad food, then how can you create good and positive emotions? If you eat "junk food," it creates indigestion and many ill effects for your body. Then how do you expect to have creative and positive emotions? We're not talking about vegetarianism versus eating meat; being a vegetarian is not necessary. But if you are talking of creative emotions, then you'll have to understand something: if you throw a piece of meat on the earth, it will not grow meat, it will only be a source of germs and bacteria. It is dead and lacks a certain life force. But if you throw down some grain or seeds, they will sprout and eventually grow other grains. So there is a difference in the quality of these foods, and you should think about that.

Just as imbalanced food can create many emotional disasters and have many negative effects on your life, so also does sex play a part in emotional balance. If the role of sex is not understood, its power in your life is very mysterious. I have observed that 99.9% of all people are controlled to some degree by the sexual urge. You need to understand the difference between food and sex: you must eat food to remain healthy, and if you don't eat food for several days, then you won't feel the sexual urge either. This means that food itself has an influence on the sexual urge. Food has a direct effect on your body; the body's needs are the most important part of your desire for food. Sex does not work like that: sexual desire occurs first in your mind. The sexual urge is born first in the mind, and if the mind doesn't feel the desire, then you won't experience it physically. When you're attracted to someone physically, you say, "I like you," because such sexual urges originate in your mind and then express themselves through the body. The desire for food, however, originates in the body, and then affects your mind.

Just as you should learn how to have good and healthy food—which means fresh, nutritious, well-balanced food—so should you also learn something about how to skillfully handle the sexual drive. This is an art that's not taught by parents. Your parents allow you to grow up; you become healthy and well-educated, and then you get married, but you still don't really know why you are married. You are not taught anything about the sexual urge or how to manage it.

In ancient times, the rishis used to teach people these things and to impart the kind of training that helps you in that area—the whole question of what sex means to you in your spiritual life. Without such an understanding, everyone in the world just thinks of sex all the time, but does not understand how to handle it. For many people, both food and sex are equally out of balance.

Next, there is another urge, the urge for sleep. Even if you are allowed to eat what you want, and to do sex when you want, if you are deprived of sleep, you will become crazy and unbalanced and won't to be able to live.

The process of sleep should also be well understood. Sleep has many stages and levels: just as you go from your living room to your kitchen, and then from the kitchen to the bedroom, so also do you go through stages of sleep. At first, you prepare yourself for sleep and yet you are not asleep.

One stage in this process is the dreaming process. You

have some faint memories and some distorted memories that come to you while you are asleep, and these are your dreams. For you, there is no doubt that they are therapeutic, but for yogis they are not therapeutic. For yogis, the small amount of time available for sleep would be reduced and robbed by dreaming, so they don't allow dreams to invade their sleep.

Dreaming is a necessity for normal people, however. Yet there is a state of deep sleep that exists when there is no content in the mind. You can go there during meditation, if you learn that method of meditation that can lead you to willful rest, and then you won't need to sleep so much.

Those who look after me sometimes wonder how I can do without sleep. It's not magic; it's that I am relaxed all the time, so why would I need more relaxation? Presently, you need relaxation because you are always on the go, physically and mentally, but if you learn to meditate and really rest, you won't need as much sleep.

As far as scientific findings are concerned, no one on the earth can really sleep for more than three consecutive hours. Actually, you sleep eight hours as a kind of tradition: it's night, there's no light out, so you go to bed. Throughout the night you wake and think, "I did not hear the alarm yet, so I'll go to sleep again," or you wake up and think, "No one called me yet, so I'll sleep some more." You have created this conditioning in your mind, so that you are in bed for no real reason, tossing and turning. You have formed a bad habit about how you handle your sleep.

I recommend that those who are really meditators, learn to wake up at three o'clock. That time of the morning is called *brahmamurta.* When you learn to wake at a specific time, then you will also learn to go to sleep—true, willful sleep. Then, you decide, "I will get up at three o'clock, so now I have to sleep," and you will simply go to sleep. After all, everything that you are is under your conscious control, or it can and *should* come under your conscious control. Presently you are not under your own conscious control, but under the control of your unconscious. Instead, your goal should be to train yourself to be under your conscious control. This is an important process.

The fourth urge is self-preservation. That means that you always desire to maintain and protect yourself; you are afraid of dying. You worry that you might die, or that someone might hurt you and you wonder who is going to look after you. Because of this negative thought pattern, you experience fear. You become a champion of negative thinking. This is the result of the urge for self-preservation. However, when you learn to surrender yourself, to surrender this individual self to the Almighty, then you are free. The happiest person in the world is one who is fearless. A fearless person is one who has no conflicts. One who has no conflicts within or without is a balanced person, and he or she is creative.

To be creative, you first have to be emotionally balanced, and to attain balance, you have to understand the negative emotions, how they arise, and how to self-counsel with them. You also have to cultivate and understand your positive emotions and then learn to express them through your mind, action, and speech. This is the beginning of learning to work creatively with your emotional nature.

Transcending Desires and Purifying the Samskaras

In the previous chapter, we described briefly the four urges for food, sex, sleep and self-preservation, and explained how they are the root-causes for negative emotions. Because of this, learning to skillfully balance and channel these urges is an important step on the spiritual path. Many people do not understand the nature of the sexual urge, the purpose of sexual relationships, or how to manage their sexuality so that it does not create obstacles on the spiritual path. Just as there is a purpose for eating food, a purpose for sleeping, and a purpose for your fears about your safety, there is also a purpose for sexuality. To make progress on the path of spirituality one needs to understand the urges, their purposes, and how to satisfy these urges.

The purpose of fear is to lead you to question and understand why you have that fear in the first place. As you examine your fears, you will learn that all your fears are somehow false and based on misunderstandings. There is no truth or reality to your fears. Many fears remain buried within you, and you never really examine them, so you remain at their mercy. In fact, you are afraid to examine your fears, but you should learn to examine each fear, one by one, and to encounter them and then be free of their control. This process is very important. Every human being has certain fears. Throughout my life, I have tried to observe and understand the way fear affects people and influences their lives.

One day in Dehra Dun, I was staying at the government house because there were no rooms elsewhere, and some people had provided me with a room there. A great and well-known woman, who was a world leader, arrived the same evening and was staying in another suite. She was famous for her courage and power, and she was not afraid of guns, and had even gone to battlefields where journalists and others were afraid. She was so brave that she inspired others. That night at twelve o'clock she began shouting and crying in her room, as though somebody was killing her, and her guards naturally were anxious outside. Their leader was crying! So I went out into the hallway and I said, "My sister, what's wrong? Why are you upset?"

And she said, "I have a very serious problem."

I said, "Tell me what's wrong, I will break down the door."

She said, "Don't do that!"

I replied, "Then open it up!"

And she said, "I can't! There is a spider on the doorknob!" So even that brave woman was afraid of spiders.

Another time, an attorney from Washington, D.C.—a strong, healthy, happy person, who helps make legislation in Congress—went to Rishikesh with some people, and stayed in one of the outside dormitories, where many people have stayed. It's a clean and comfortable place, but one night the attorney started screaming. So I came out and said, "What's the matter?" And the attorney screamed, "There is a lizard in here!" In tropical countries like India, there are small lizards everywhere, but they are harmless and don't bite or cause any problems. Other people are afraid of snakes. Everyone has a variety of fears.

This even happened to me. I was so afraid of snakes that I used to check my pockets all the time, because I was worried that somehow, a snake might get into my pocket. Whenever I stayed in a hotel, in any room, even in America on the eleventh floor, I used to check the pillows and bedding for snakes. When I first came to this country, that fear continued, and my Master helped me with those fears at that time.

Everyone has fears. The urge that is the root of these fears is the desire for self-preservation. Of course, you desire to preserve and protect yourself, but you should also understand your urges in a little greater depth: why are you an individual? Were you created merely to remain a separate individual?

The desires for both self-preservation and sex have important roles in your life. Why does a human being become so involved in sexual desire and activity that he thinks only about that? One reason is that there are two varieties of joy in life. One is called *bishiya ananda,* the kind of joy that you obtain when you do sex; such joy does not last very long. You want it to last forever; you don't want merely five minutes of joy and then the sadness that you experience, but that is what happens to you. Anything in the world that you enjoy or that gives you joy does not really last for a very long time. Such joy is fleeting: the object that gives you joy or pleasure, the object which becomes a reason for you to live or act—that object itself changes. There is no object on the earth that does not change, that does not go through the process of change, death, and decay. So it is impossible for such objects to give you lasting joy. You cannot count on them.

Your relationships with the objects of your sexual desire also change, and when you remain floating on the level of sexual joy alone—and fail to understand that there is something deeper in a human being, when you don't understand your life on the deeper levels, and when you do not communicate with another beyond the level of the body—then that causes problems. Such relationships do not last for very long.

It's a natural human urge to want to be happy all the time. It's a goal of human life to obtain happiness, and the sexual life gives pleasure and joy for a moment, but it does not last forever. A human being is really seeking that joy and happiness which is perennial and constant.

You do not know how to attain that perennial happiness because when you examine and experience the joys of the world—deriving joy from first one source and then another source, going from one object to another—you are disappointed. Finally, you turn within. Then you go to the subtler realms and seek to understand the meaning of life, and you learn that it's not possible for you to attain that perennial happiness and joy in the external world, with such fleeting objects. When you go beyond these objects, then you finally find joy in the Center of Consciousness within.

So the reason for sexual relationships is for their joy, but you need to understand the higher goals beyond that goal. In India, we often use a Persian word *shadi* which means "happiness" or "marriage." When you get married, your spouse gives you a ring, which symbolizes something: the two separate ends of the same piece of metal come together and that becomes a perfect complete circle, a ring. Your purpose is to be united to the end of life, and that is a kind of completion or happiness.

Happiness is the ultimate goal. All your actions in the world—whether you eat your food, get married or have children, homes or friends—these all exist for your happiness. But do these objects of the world give us that complete happiness? They offer the best of joys—for a moment—but not everlasting happiness. You find their joy and then again you return to the same world of conflict, sadness, sorrow, and worry. Human union gives you a joy that is a glimpse, a foretaste that there is something higher, which is everlasting.

Human relationships could be truly joyous; they could create a great and complete happiness, if two human beings really understood and accepted each other, and learned how to follow the spiritual path together. All the great religions repeat one message: that God is the principle of equality, love, peace, and happiness, within and without, which is omnipresent, omniscient, and omnipotent. If that is true, then who are you and from where did you come? You live in that love and peace; you have come from that. So that love, peace, and happiness are within you, too.

When you go to that Source within, and you see that Light in your partner, then you realize, "My partner is not a mere body or an object of sensory gratification, but a human being who has that Light of Divinity within." When both partners realize that, then your relationship is a complete temple. When you understand that a human being is a shrine, then you don't need to go to an external temple, church or chapel to pray. That experience is love: love means knowing the Truth within. Then, suddenly, you will discover yourself giving all that you have without any condition, because you have understood the Truth. Without love, there is no meaning.

I have met many messengers and many prophets of Truth, but I have met few prophets of Love. Those who do not mingle their path with religious fanaticism always learn to serve others. The great men on the earth have one common characteristic: selflessness and dedication in their mind, behavior, and speech. As we mentioned earlier, it would have been easy for Christ to have said "I'm sorry. Why do you want to crucify me? I will not do what angers you any more." He could easily have done that to escape death, but he did not, because he was dedicated to what he was doing. He knew what he was doing and he was committed to it. He did not fear his crucifixion, because He was one with Truth.

In the same way, Moses remained all alone without food and water on the mountain for many days, because he knew that there is something special that a human being has to attain. He was born for that and he had to do it. All the world's great men and women have had this characteristic of selflessness, and all also understood the law of karma, no matter which religion they followed. The Christians say, "As you sow, so shall you reap," and the Buddhists recognize the same truth. Buddhism is built on the foundation of the law of karma. The Hindus, too, believe this principle, and it is contained in the Koran, as well.

There is no "forgiveness" in this law; there is no escape from its consequences. If you have sown the seed of an apple, you won't reap a guava. But the human being is a peculiar creature and then he says to God, "O Lord, I have sown an apple seed, now please create a guava with it!"

Human beings behave in that way out of human weakness; it's the result of human ego and ignorance. Ignorance is the mother of all your problems, pains, and miseries. Ignorance creates all your fears. You are afraid of someone because he or she is different from you. The day that you and that person, creature or object become one, then you will no longer be afraid. Of what are you afraid? There is only one Reality; all your fears will last and will create problems for you only as long as you separate yourself and isolate yourself from the Truth that is manifested around you.

To be free from all fear means to be one with the Truth. Once you know the Truth, you are free. Then you know that this person you fear has the same Center of Consciousness that you have, so you are not afraid of the person. The great sages in their forest dwellings have made experiments on the subject of human fear. Even ferocious animals, such as tigers and snakes, will not hurt or harm you, if you know the Truth.

I, myself, had this experience once not because I was a great or powerful sage, but still, such a thing happened to me. I was in silence in the mountains and I was very tired. It was about three o'clock in the afternoon, and by nature, I get sleepy at three o'clock because I don't sleep at night. In the daytime after lunch I have a habit of taking a nap. So this day, I got tired at three o'clock, but I still had to climb another four miles. I had already climbed five miles, and I rested, ate some food and water for my lunch, and then found a cave and went inside. I was so sleepy that I lay down right there. I had a kind of poncho blanket that I put over myself and soon I was half asleep.

Gradually, I realized that something was crawling over my body and scratching me. Two small tiger cubs were playing and making noise. My eyelids were very heavy, but this was not a dream. I said to myself, "Oh no, they are tiger cubs! What will happen when their mother comes?" This thought came into my mind, but I was very tired, so I went to sleep. They thought that I was their mother, and they were scratching, running around, and licking me. I could not really sleep in that situation, but I tried to.

This lasted for about half an hour and suddenly I saw something shadow-like in front of the cave. I opened my eyes and saw a tigress standing there, waiting to come in. I did not have any weapon, so I thought, "I'm not hurting your cubs. I don't have any intention to harm you. If you move aside, I will go out and you can come in." That's exactly what happened: she stood aside, and I went out, and then she came into her cave. There is a simple saying in the *Ramayana* that is true: even the smallest of creatures and animals understand what's right and what is wrong.

There are three major kinds of knowledge and ways of knowing: instincts, sense perceptions, and intuition. Animals are basically guided by their instincts, and most of their behavior is the result of instincts, not knowledge. For example, there is a part of the ocean called the "ocean desert," which does not contain much food, so sea animals do not generally remain there, because there is nothing to eat. If you place a young turtle that was just born there, that turtle will start swimming toward the shore by instinct.

Human beings also have instincts. Instinct is one of the sources of knowledge. Humans also have several different sources of knowledge: sense perception is a second source, and sometimes there is also a "sixth sense." Sometimes all your five senses suddenly become concentrated—that is called the sixth sense, and then you *know* something will occur, and you know that you know. You are absolutely sure, and then it happens. Something happens suddenly and you say, "I knew it would happen a few months ago." This happens to everyone to some degree. This is called a "hunch." Hunches roll down from the heights of intuition, the finest of all the kinds of knowledge that we have. We have a beautiful library within, our "intuitive library." The highest of all knowledge comes from that library, and once you have that knowledge, you don't need any sensory evidence: you *know*. Thus, there are three main streams of knowledge: knowledge received through instinct, knowledge received through the senses, and knowledge received through intuition.

Our instincts include the urges for food, sex, sleep, and self-preservation. They are primitive fountains, very primitive urges. When you consider an emotion, if you quietly sit down and examine it carefully, you'll eventually realize that the emotion is somehow related to one of the urges. If you are overeating, it could be because something is wrong with your sexual adjustment. This is because there is a process of compensation and replacement in the body and the emotional life.

In America I've observed things that I have not seen anywhere else: here, there is no such thing as repair, but there is certainly replacement! If a wife and husband fight, there's no such thing as repairing the relationship; they each just look for replacements. You do not understand how to adjust and adapt within yourself and in your relationships. In your daily life, you need to remember that contentment is your goal. You want to be contented, and to be happy and contented you need to learn how to adjust to others. If you know how to adjust yourself to others, you'll be content, but if you want to be content and happy without understanding how to adjust, you will never experience that.

You need to adjust your mind, actions, and speech so that they are compatible with others, whose mind, action, and speech do not relate exactly to yours. You'll find that you have problems doing this, but at the same time, if you follow this process, you'll also find that you become free and contented.

You should allow your good thoughts to be expressed through your actions. Many times your good thoughts are not fully expressed. In this manner you constantly damage and kill that sensitive inner part of you which would help to bring about your own enlightenment and growth. Then, a time comes when something negative has been built up inside you, because you are constantly hurting yourself, which is the greatest of all sins. The only real sin in life is to kill your own conscience. If you do not kill your conscience then you'll never commit mistakes, because your conscience will guide you wisely. But the more mistakes you commit, and the more you blame and condemn yourself, the more you hurt your conscience. The conscience is the clear mirror within you; it is not your mind, urges or your emotions. Don't allow your conscience to be enveloped by the dust of ignorance, and don't shatter or damage your conscience, but keep it clear by listening to it. The conscience is very helpful in dealing with your mind and its problems.

In the Christian tradition, as we said, Saul was transformed and became Paul, because one day he listened to

his conscience and understood that the path he was following was not the right path. Then he became a sage. In
your case, however, you often knowingly continue to do
things that are wrong. You know that one course of action
is right, and yet you do not do it—which is a sin against
your own conscience. When you know that something is
right, and yet you go against it, you act against your own
conscience, and that weakens you. To act against your own
conscience kills the powerful force within you, your determination and willpower. If you kill your willpower, you
can never be dynamic; your dynamic will will depart. You
know what is right for you, and yet you often go on
repeating wrong action. This is a crime, and there is no
remedy for it. You know that something is bad for your
growth, and yet you constantly repeat it, because of your
bad habits.

You need to put into practice this teaching: first, you
need to understand what you are doing wrong. Next, you
need to create new grooves for your mind, so that your
mind does not automatically flow in its old grooves, but
instead begins to flow in the new grooves. Learn to counsel
yourself and have a self-dialogue. Learn to mentally talk to
yourself. Sit down and have a dialogue with yourself; ask
yourself why you are doing an action. Many times you will
say to yourself, "I don't want to do this, but I have been
doing it, so now it's a routine," and then you'll understand
the process of habit formation. With all your idealization
of sadhana and gurus and teachers, you have neglected one
thing: you need to know something practical. You need to
know a practical method of gaining freedom from those
weaknesses that you have formed in your childhood, which
have become part of your life, and are difficult for you to
resolve.

Learn to work with yourself: all your actions are
controlled by your thoughts, and all your thoughts are
controlled by your emotions. By comparison with your

emotions, thought has little power, but if you can use your emotional power constructively, you can channel it and attain ecstasy. Then, emotions can become creative. Your emotional power can be utilized in a creative way and can lead you to a height of Oneness, which will give you real happiness.

There have been many great people in the world, such as Chaitanya Mahaprabhu, Ramakrishna Paramahansa, Saint Bernard, and Saint Teresa, who were great sages. They all used their emotional power, rather than the power of mind. This is called the "path of heart," rather than the path of the mind. To follow the path of mind is very dangerous, because it's like the sharp edge of a knife. If you make a mistake with your mind, you will be destroyed, but if you learn to use your emotion positively, you can attain the highest of joys and happiness.

Now we come to the issue of "desires." From where does desire arise, and what is the nature of desire? As we discussed previously, the prime desire and the origin of all other desires is kama. Kama is the mother of every desire, and it motivates you to do anything and everything. Kama is blind desire; it has no sense of discrimination, judgment or understanding. It motivates you to do something simply to fulfill that desire—because it exists.

As we discussed, when kama is not fulfilled, you get angry and frustrated—that is krodha, the emotion of anger. When you are angry, then you are completely blind. If you compare yourself to a dog, you will realize that even a dog never loses its temper in the way that you do. When you are frustrated, when your desires are not fulfilled, you can even hurt your child or your wife whom you love so much.

But if this desire of kama is fulfilled, then you become proud, and the fulfillment of the desire feeds your pride, which is the emotion called muda. Your mind thinks, "I have achieved my desire!" This is intoxicating, and when you are under the influence of this intoxication, you do not think clearly and you behave badly.

If your desire is fulfilled, you compare yourself with others and think, "I now have it, and you don't have the object. I have it and I am proud of it! This is mine because I have it. It is not yours." This is lobha, or greed. Lobha motivates you to feel: "This is mine and I don't want to share it with you. It's my house. My house has twelve rooms, I have only one child, and the rest of the rooms are empty, but I won't allow you to stay here. It's my house." That is greed. It further separates you from others.

Next, you start comparing your home with the one someone else owns, and then you become jealous. You think, "Does someone have a better house? Oh, no, my house is much better." You begin to compare yourself with others, and then you become puffed up with pride, and you go on living this way, feeding your ego. On the other hand, if you feel your home is not so nice, you identify with feelings of inadequacy and depression. Thus, the original mother of the whole process of developing negative emotions is desire.

At some point, you begin to wonder how you can transcend your desires. Consider what you are actually doing through your actions: you try to fulfill your desires, one after another, like crazy people. You repeat the same actions every day, trying to fulfill the desire, and yet it is never fulfilled. Your actions just put more fuel on the fire of your desire.

This is the process: you want to fulfill a desire. You have the desire, so naturally the desire will motivate you to fulfill it. This entire process of desire drives you crazy and creates your emotional problems. You want to fulfill the desire, and you are doing something to try to fulfill it, but in a few days' time you will discover that your desire is still not fulfilled. So then, you go on to another desire, and in this way you make your unconscious mind into a basement junkyard. You have been doing this kind of unconscious experiment with all your desires, but such experiments have already been done a long time ago by the great sages. You should follow their advice: the great sages taught that you can never attain anything truly great by fulfilling desires alone. You have to understand this point to make progress. Attaining objects alone can never make you happy; the question is, how do we attain a state that is free of desire?

It's not extremely easy, but neither is it impossible, to attain a state that is free from desires. However, even while you still have desires, you can be happier if you understand how to reconcile these. At present, you try to fulfill your desires through your actions. It is not your actions that actually make you unhappy. Doing actions is your birthright, and you cannot live without action. You are caught in a trap: a human being cannot live without performing action, but when he performs the action, he then has to reap the fruits of his action—that's a certainty. When the person reaps the fruits of his actions, then those fruits again motivate him to do further actions.

For example, perhaps a couple build a home with a budget of $80,000. Both the wife and husband are very happy with the beautiful house. Even the neighbors know it is a beautiful house, but there is nothing inside, because they did not have money budgeted for the carpet and furnishings. So now, they desire to acquire those things, and soon they have developed desire after desire. You have one pillow cover, and now you need two or three to replace it. You need dolls for the children's rooms. The children grow and now they need a pet dog. So on it goes, and there is no end to it. You are caught in the snare of desires and you cannot come out of that.

You should have desires—you *do* have desires—and you cannot live without having things. But you need to learn a way to be unaffected and live above this level, even though you have desires. There is a way to accomplish that, and it is called the path of action or the path of karma. You can follow this path if you know how to perform your actions with the right mindfulness. You cannot live without performing actions; no human being can possibly do that.

Your ancestors, the great sages, said to let all your actions become duties. Actions become duties when you understand that you are really doing this action for another—for your wife or child or neighbor or country or for humanity. Actions become duties because you accept a responsibility to do them.

If you think, "This person is my wife, so I should do certain things for her," then any action that you perform with that awareness becomes your duty. Unfortunately, then you think that your duty makes you a slave. I've known housewives who felt burdened by the pressure of their duties, and when I say, "Why don't you sit down and have a cup of tea and relax," they protest, "I have to go home; I am married. The children will come home from school soon. I have to be there."

So they feel that they are acting under the pressure of their duties all day, and when you feel that, then your duties make you a slave. Here is an impasse: you cannot live without doing your duties, but then you feel like a slave. There are several points to remember: first, you cannot live without doing actions, and then, secondly, you always receive the fruits of actions. Third, you cannot live without doing your duties, and fourth, the wrong attitude toward your duty makes you a slave. Then how can you be free?

There is one important skill that you need to learn to be free. You create everything out of a desire for *love*. You always create and act for some purpose. You think, "I wish my husband loved me," or "I wish my wife loved me; she never expresses it to me." Sometimes people get divorced because the love is not expressed. Many times, both people are wonderful. Why does one couple live together happily when another couple does not, although they are all good people?

None of you know how to really express your love. You create and act for love your whole life. There is no animal or creature who does not crave love, and love means attention. Meditation, too, is attention; without attention, you cannot meditate. The word "meditation" comes from the same root as "medical," and that is the way a doctor should attend to his patients—seriously, lovingly, and selflessly.

So you create and act for love all the time. You say, "If I have love, I can live in a gutter with somebody, but if I have everything else but have no love, I wouldn't want to live in a castle." What is that love which you crave? What do you mean by love, and how can you find it? If I ask you to describe what you seek, you will fail: you cannot describe love itself. Whenever you try to describe love, you end up describing actions, because you cannot explain what love itself is. Sometimes you can express your love without any speech or any action, but through your feelings alone.

When you are in love, you use a peculiar language and you may make gestures which are not normal in other situations, but they are accepted by those you love. You may tease someone or make a funny face if you are in love with someone, and the other person will like it, but if you did it publicly with another person, they would be offended. The most ancient language in the world is the language of love. This language doesn't lie or misinform or distort the world, unlike the other languages we use for manners or politeness. The words of other languages become empty; those empty words have no heart or love.

As we indicated earlier, as you perform your actions and make them into duties, your actions will make you a slave, unless you do them with love. Learn to "grease" your duties with love. Love is the one thing that can help keep you from being a slave to your duties.

In the Western hemisphere everyone has a job. No one values their job because they think they can easily get another. You are confident about that—if a doctor does not want to do medicine, he can leave and become a carpenter the next day. But in other countries this cannot happen, because they don't have such an open economy, and it's difficult to get jobs. Here, even though you have freedom, everyone is unhappy, and you do things which you do not really want to do, yet you persist doing them. This creates a constant conflict in your mind, and that constant conflict is the source of unhappiness.

You say, "I only do this job because I have to pay the rent and taxes and I have to buy food—that's why I do it. Otherwise, I wouldn't do this work." So you do things which you do not want to do—that's why you are unhappy and experience stress all the time. The cause of stress is that you don't want to do your duties, yet you are forced to do so, and so you do them but you resent them. It is your attitude that you have to change: you need to learn to do your duties with a spirit of love and joy.

Any urge that is incorrectly expressed will also create stress: if you are not hungry and you force yourself to eat, you are overeating, and it will create stress. If you don't really understand the goal of sexuality, but you do sex to try to release tension or satisfy your ego through sex, that will create stress for you, because you are doing something without the right attitude. Eating food or engaging in sexuality without the right attitude will not give you satisfaction; it will not give you any real joy.

When you cannot handle something in your daily life, you often want to go to sleep. But when you do that, you are not really sleeping—you will just have nightmares. Again, what really creates stress is having no love within yourself. When you have lost touch with the love within—which is the very source and very essence—then you experience stress. Naturally you will feel stress if you do not grease your duties with love; then, you'll always be un-happy. If, however, you learn to do your duties with love, then whatever you do is fine. In fact, if you do everything with love, then life is wonderful! Then, life is a poem; it's poetry, it's a song—so learn to do your duties with love. You say, "I live with my husband because we have kids," but that's not the right attitude; learn to live with him with love.

You can learn to create such love. Love is a creation of human beings; it does not drop suddenly from the heavens above. The highest of all human creations is love. Love is consideration, caring, sharing, surrendering, and giving. Love itself means giving. Whomever you love, decide one important thing: that you will not hurt that person, through your mind, action or speech. Ahimsa (non-violence) is the expression of love; they are one and the same. Learn to express love; learn to cultivate that attitude toward others.

We all have homes, and our homes are meant for our inner spiritual experiments with ourselves. Our homes are laboratories, and when we learn something about love in our homes, then we can go out and do useful things in the community and the world. But if we fail at home, then we really fail. And, there is still another home, a personal laboratory within yourself. You are learning how to live with others, but how can you really live with others when you are not happy with yourself? You are not yet happy because of your desires. You do not know how to attenuate those desires. You should have desires; you cannot become swamis, *sannyasis*, or renunciates, renouncing all your desires. Renunciation itself is not so important; what is important is learning to live in the world, yet remain unaffected. No matter who you are, whether you're a swami or an ordinary man in the world, you should learn the technique of living in the world, yet remaining un-affected.

Do not forget that this life is only a journey, and you

are a traveler. On this journey, you must have something solid for yourself, like an anchor or a firm rudder. If you lose your rudder, your boat will float aimlessly and you won't know where it is going. Your rudder in life is to remember that you are on a journey, and that this world is not your home.

A seeker should think, "I am only a guest here in this world. A guest cannot afford to be absurd with the host. What right have I to misbehave or to be greedy? I am on a journey and I must complete my journey." This life is like a very crowded procession, and you have to see that you don't hurt anyone, and neither are you hurt. To achieve that you must learn to be skillful. Learn the skill of performing your actions, yet remaining free from reaping the fruits. That is accomplished when you cultivate the attitude of love.

Often people ask how long it will take for them to be liberated, and I answer, "One second!" The whole world could be liberated and happy in one day's time, if all human beings decided to do something very rational and logical: if I perform an action, I am bound to reap the fruits of the actions, and if you do an action, you are also bound to reap the fruits of your action. We are not caught by our actions, but by their fruits. But if I do my actions with love for you, and at the same time you do your actions with love for me, then we are both free. Humans have not yet learned this skill; humanity has not yet learned to do things for others, selflessly and lovingly. That's why the sages say that love liberates, and that love is real knowledge. Learn to do things for others because learning to act in this way liberates you.

When you learn to do things for others, there are four aspects to the process: you learn to give; you learn to love; you learn to be free; and you learn to follow the law of karma. If you do not learn this process, you cannot ever attenuate your many desires. As we noted earlier, all the strains of your negative emotions arise in some fashion from the primitive fountains. You need to learn to understand these primitive fountains and their effect on you. In order to do that, you need to learn to observe your mind and to counsel with yourself. Then, you can be free of the burden and unhappiness created by your own desires. Having examined in some depth the issue of desires, let us return now to discuss the role of samskaras.

The subject of samskaras is a large, important, and comprehensive one. You who are students of yoga, often talk about samskaras, but you don't really understand this term, and so you simply use the concept of samskaras as an excuse for your personal problems. For example, if I ask someone, "Why did you divorce your wife?" the person may reply, "It's just my samskaras." People say they have an accident or a disease or any problem and that it's just due to samskaras, but saying this does not help you, because you don't know what you really mean, and you don't accept the responsibility for understanding yourself.

You need to clearly understand the difference between habits and samskaras. Samskaras motivate you to do something again and again. Your samskaras are the accumulation of impressions, the merits and demerits that are stored in the conscious and unconscious mind. You do not have control over your samskaras.

Your body is related to your mind and your thinking process, with the help of two guards, the two aspects of breath, exhalation and inhalation. The mind itself has two levels: the first is the conscious level of mind that you educate in your daily life, at colleges or at home. The other level of mind is the unconscious aspect of mind, which you are also simultaneously educating. Certainly, you should get a good education and learn to educate the conscious part of your mind that you use in the waking state, and then you may also derive some unconscious benefit. But the part of mind that you do not consciously educate is

referred to as "the sleeping mind" or "the dreaming mind."
It is not under your control. This vast part of your mind
remains uncultured, untrained, and uneducated.

That vast level of mind is the unconscious. Great men
know how to expand their conscious level of mind, and
then there is nothing that remains unconscious for them.
They expand the field of the conscious mind and reduce
the unconscious. The sages are conscious of that which is
unconscious for you. For them, there is no such thing as
the past, present, and future. For you, there are only the
past and the future, because you have no present awareness; you do not live now. Your past impressions come
forward constantly in your minds and motivate you to
perform new actions in the present. When this isn't the
case, then you are thinking about the future, so you seldom
live in the here and now. In meditation the sages say that
there is no sense of time. Meditation annihilates time and
then you are free, and you can be here and now. That's why
they tell us, "Meditate, meditate, meditate!"

Whatever you do, hear or see, an impression is stored
in the unconscious mind. There are many layers and levels
to the unconscious. Perhaps one day you feel very happy,
and you think, "I feel great! I have no anxiety," and then
suddenly a samskara bubble arises in your mind, and you
suddenly become miserable.

There are many layers and levels of samskaras, the
impressions of your actions and desires, asleep in your
unconscious. These samskaras become active every now
and then, and then they motivate and control your mind
and your emotions.

The mind alone cannot do anything by itself. The mind
has no power to take in information by itself if the senses
are not focused on it. If your eyes are not directed toward
something, the mind cannot see or perceive it. The mind
employs the senses of hearing, seeing, tasting, touching,
and smelling. These are the five cognitive senses. There are

also another five gross senses: the mouth, the hands and feet, and the organs of elimination and generation. Thus, there are a total of ten senses.

The mind functions through those senses. Whenever an event takes place that relates to an impression in your mind, then the impression or samskara becomes active. The conscious mind is actually controlled by the unconscious, and that's why we human beings cannot easily make progress. You know how to culture and cultivate only a small part of your mind, but a vast part of the mind remains unknown to you. All your actions leave some impression in your unconscious mind, and those impressions then become your samskaras and control your life. To make progress, your samskaras need to be purified.

You can do that in meditation by asking all the impressions in your mind to come forward, so that you can examine and burn them. Swamis wear saffron-colored garb to symbolize the color of fire, the color of knowledge. When you have the determination, "I have burnt all my desires in the fire of knowledge," then you wear that color. You can consciously bring forward all the latent, buried impressions during meditation, telling your mind that you are ready to face them, and if you have built that kind of determination and willpower, you can allow those samskaras to be burnt mentally. They are all mental impressions, there is nothing solid or material there. All these past impressions can be burnt, and then you can be free from them. The goal is to expand the conscious aspect of mind so that there is no unconscious.

There are actually two known ways to purify your samskaras, the impressions that you have stored in your lifetime. But there are also only two known ways to happiness: either you fulfill your desires and understand which desires you want to fulfill by doing your duties, or otherwise you completely renounce the desire, and then reduce your desires to a minimum. When you come to the point where there is no desire, then there is nothing to be fulfilled. You have two choices of path: fulfill the desire or renounce the desire. When you fulfill your desires by doing actions, you must remember that to do so, you must do your actions with love.

You can also burn your samskaras. To burn your samskaras, you sit in deep meditation, build your determination, and tell your mind and your samskaras, "At this time my mind is only for meditation. I have to meditate and learn to go beyond this mire of delusion and confusion created by my mind." Then, you allow all the impressions to come forward and you don't get involved with them. That method is called "inspection within," or introspection, and slowly you learn to become a witness. This is one method.

Another method is to burn your samskaras inside that fire of knowledge and to offer all those samskaras to the Light, to that great fire within, and then burn them. These are the two methods.

Modern people think that they know many sciences and that they are very wise but inside, they are very lonely and afraid. Their pockets are full of pills and their homes are dispensaries. They have huge locks on their doors; they are fearful people, because there is nothing inside themselves. They have no anchor in life, and their movements are not free.

How can you enjoy such a life? If you live under the pressure of such fear all the time, how is it possible for you to enjoy life? You do not enjoy it and you cannot enjoy it, because of your fears of losing what you have, and of not gaining what you desire. These two fears constantly haunt your happiness.

To have inner strength you first need to really accept that you are on a journey in life. When you are on a journey, you travel light; you don't carry everything that you have at home. You take just enough money for the trip. That's the principle: to have enough money means to have inner wisdom. Travelling light means not to have any anxieties or burdens in your daily life.

A good formula for happiness is to remember that all the things of the world are for you to have and use—that's why you have them. You commit a mistake in thinking that you *own* them, but you also do not use them productively. Nature and reality will punish you if you try to own the things of the world but do not use them for your growth. Learn to use all the things of the world; they are for you, but they are not yours. Don't seek to possess things; possessing anything is very dangerous because it creates attachment.

Nothing external can help you to attain the reality of Truth. A rich man looks at a poor man and thinks, "This poor man has nothing but he is very happy." And the poor man looks at the rich man, and thinks that he has everything, and envies him. Both are unhappy. You know that the external world—the world of means—cannot make you happy. It makes you comfortable, and often when you are comfortable, you forget the purpose of life. Do not forget that the purpose of life is to attain freedom from all misery and pain.

To attain happiness you don't have to travel, leave your home, or abandon your duties. This is the message from the great sages of the Himalayas. Remain at home and do your duties. Learn to do your duties lovingly and decrease your attachments. Use the word love, so that you learn to give. Attachments contract your personality; love expands it. Purify your samskaras so that the samskaras do not disturb your actions and speech, and then cultivate or accept in your mind only those desires which you can fulfill and which do not create problems for you.

Chapter 6

Developing
Strength and Willpower

In order to make progress in any aspect of life, it is essential to develop your willpower and your personal strength. Often, however, when you decide to develop your willpower, you may resolve to do dramatic things, but this can actually cause problems for you, because if you cannot yet do what you resolve, then you will find that your strength and your willpower are being damaged rather than developed.

If you sincerely want to develop personal strength and willpower, you should first learn to keep yourself open and be an observer of yourself until you observe that your willpower has become dynamic. Instead of making such dramatic resolutions, simply make yourself open to observing yourself and decide to experiment in observing yourself.

When you do such experiments with yourself, your resolutions and deeds should not hurt others. If you try to do something for yourself but end up hurting others, that is actually a very selfish act. When you do not want to share the fruits and positive results of your deeds with others, that is also self-centered. You can divide and analyze all your actions and expressions into many types and categories, but once a day you should simply try to do small things for your children, spouse or friends. You should do very small simple things for others, and you will find that it helps you very much.

Thus far in your life, you usually have put yourself first and done things first for yourself. You think, "I need this; I want this. I like to do this, and I am going to do it because I want to." For example, you may be sitting at the breakfast table, and you simply grab something for yourself and start to eat it without having any consideration or thoughtfulness for your partner. Just for the sake of experimentation with your self-centeredness, try instead to be a little bit courteous. If you do that, you'll find that your whole home life changes. Try giving a plate of food to your partner first. Nothing will happen to diminish you; you will not lose out on anything and you will not be deprived of food, but you will observe an effect in yourself.

If you want to strengthen yourself, try to develop consideration for others and see how much you can do for them. Usually you do things only for yourself and you also expect others to do things for you. If you develop and cultivate in yourself the desire to give to others, and then once a day do that without any selfishness, you will be surprised to find that you will enjoy everything more.

So far, you have tasted only one-sided pleasures: you think of yourself and then you try to enjoy things for yourself. You don't know how others are experiencing those things or whether they are enjoying them or not. You usually just weigh others' enjoyment through your own enjoyment. But if you really consider others and think about their feelings with consideration, then your whole experience of life changes—you will discover a new kind of joy.

Your thought power—the power of your mind and its thoughts—is the most important power you have within you, and it is the point from which all communication originates. If you develop in yourself thoughts of serving others, helping them, and showing genuine consideration and kindness, then you will find that a dynamic change takes place in your relationships. When you think only of yourself and decide that you want to do something no matter what happens, then you are caught by your selfishness and only misery results.

Selfishness is your biggest enemy. Throughout history man has been applying all his resources, trying to conquer this enemy called selfishness. He cannot completely do this; he has not accomplished it yet. And those few who have really conquered their selfishness have not ever been understood accurately by other people. Look at the lives of Jesus and Moses: they did nothing for themselves, but how many people really understood them? When they wanted to communicate the most profound teachings of spirituality to people, then, out of millions of people, only a few came to the mountain where this advanced knowledge was being imparted.

Slowly you should prepare yourself for this level of teaching. Knowledge will come of itself, but all knowledge really comes from within. It is already within you. If you remember the story of Isaac Newton, who discovered the law of gravity, then you may recall that according to the story, an apple fell one day and he suddenly understood the principle of gravity. But apples fall down every day and usually we do not discover anything. Newton actually discovered this law from within. The real source of knowledge is within; the world outside only gives you facts to relate to that particular knowledge that is already within you. Never forget that the source of knowledge is within you. You should also never forget that your conscience needs cleansing every day.

Learn to depend only on inner knowledge. Your mind plays tricks with you, and then you suddenly begin to lose your self-confidence. The moment you lose your self-confidence, then your mind cannot decide about anything on time. If you miss doing what you should have done today, and try instead to do it tomorrow, it is not the same.

Great men know how to decide things on time; they are the most successful people in the world. This is true from a mundane, worldly point of view, and it is also true from a divine point of view. The key to all success in life lies in having developed your decisive faculty so that you can use it in your daily life.

You may wonder how you can accomplish this. If you go around experiencing self-inflicted pain all day and you do not try to control yourself, to mend your ways, or to change your habits, then you will not receive much benefit from life. You should surrender everywhere else in life, but you should never surrender to your own negative habits; you should go on fighting this battle and continue it your whole life. This is not a one-day battle, and the day that you accept defeat in working with yourself is the day you are really gone from the platform of life.

Do not accept defeat from either adversity outside yourself or from your own negative thinking—go on and you will overcome them. That is possible to achieve through willpower; you have that willpower. The more one-pointed your mind becomes, the more concentrated the mind is, and then your willpower will become even more dynamic.

If you have an accident, or face a threat or extreme adversity, you use your whole knowledge and your whole being. There is something within that helps you at such times, and that means that your mind has a center. By knowing the Center within yourself you can help yourself. You are not limited to being a body alone; you are not limited to being the mind alone. You are actually very great, but you know only a small part of yourself—you do not know the greatest and highest part of yourself.

The greatest and highest part of you is God; the lowest part is the body. At present, you know only your body—you think that the body is you and that you are the body.

But when you understand that God is within you, that the Power of powers is within you, then you are free from your limitations.

None of the problems that you face today is really created by anybody outside yourself. Whatever emotional problem you have, however, it is related to something or someone else outside you. If you analyze the problem, you will realize that you have yourself created it. You really do not have any innate problems, but you are in the habit of creating problems for yourself. You learn to create problems for yourself, and then you confuse others and create problems for them as well. Many of your problems involve how you relate to somebody else outside yourself. This means that you create problems for yourself through your relationships.

If you want to solve your problems in life, you need to learn to adjust in your relationships. For example, you can solve the problems that you have with your wife in your own mind. You could easily accomplish that, but unfortunately your personality is usually so involved in the problem that you cannot get away from your egocentric ideas. The force of your ego is so strong that no matter how many counselors you see or how many times you pray, nothing improves. No matter how many times someone communicates something to you, nothing helps you. But if you really have an interest in knowing and learning something about yourself, then you will finally learn it. The whole secret of learning is not to fight yourself, but to simply allow yourself to know. To do that, you need to create a real and sincere motivation for self-improvement.

Create an interest and motivation to understand the things that are taking place before you: whatever you do, do it with genuine interest. Why do people like to think about something before they do it? Because *doing* itself is not very important; the enjoyment is not in the action. The action itself is only an expression of your enjoyment. There is a difference: when you do an action it is not actually a process of enjoyment, it is only an expression of enjoyment. The real enjoyment of something lies in your mind and heart alone.

Sometimes you think of something very soothing, and you enjoy thinking this thought, even though the action itself is not taking place then. Sometimes you do what you consider to be the best and most enjoyable of all acts, but you do not fully enjoy being there, because your mind is somewhere else.

Learn to enjoy whatever you do with both mental and physical coordination. This will happen when you create a real and sincere interest for the things that you are doing. All your duties—whether they are smaller or larger, higher or more trivial—should be done with interest and attention.

Those who are married should consider this: a wife and husband may go to bed without having the real intention to enjoy each other, but merely to do something to please the other. Perhaps the woman may think that her husband will be happy if she gives him sex, or he may think that he's giving his love to his wife. When this happens, they are both only imitating something. They are not insincere, but neither are they being fully honest with themselves in such a situation. Such an act is not fulfilling and it causes strain within yourself; such strain may create disturbances, such as physical problems. This happens because people do things without real interest, without real love, or without total will—when they simply imitate.

When you do something selflessly for someone else, you should also *enjoy* doing that. If you say, "I am doing this selflessly," but your mind is actually somewhere else, then that is not really a selfless act. That is doing something half-heartedly, absentmindedly, and without any true interest. Learn to enjoy things. You enjoy some things, but you do not know the true art of enjoyment. Learn to enjoy things by putting your whole heart and mind into them, and then you will really enjoy them. If doing something strains you, then you should realize that somewhere within, either your body, mind, or heart does not fully agree, and that is why you are stressed.

What I am trying to make clear is that although we think we can do the actions of our daily lives selflessly, they are not really good for our physical and psychological health if true positive interest is not created. If we do not do things wholeheartedly we do not enjoy them, no matter how much selfless action we try to do.

The biggest joy in life is enjoying the things that you do for others. If others enjoy the act, but you are thinking only about yourself and not about the other, then that is a small and petty enjoyment. You will experience the highest enjoyment when you are doing something selflessly for others, yet you are at the same time fully enjoying that so-called selfless act.

Sometimes people are able to do exceptional things for their spouse—for example, they can actually endure pain for the sake of their spouse—but they cannot do that for others. You can learn to do things for others and for the world in the same way that the great people, such as Buddha, Christ, and Krishna did. You can expand yourself and slowly become great by doing your duties and enjoying the way you do your duties. This level of higher enjoyment is possible in the world.

Here is another secret: if you have no duties, you may think of yourself as a happy man, but then there is no real test of your strength. The real test of your strength is when you are tested in the world of your relationships. The more you isolate yourself, the more you contract your personality. The more you expand, selflessly and with interest in others' welfare, the more you enjoy life.

I see two extremes in your society. Some people are very self-centered, and their personalities contract, and eventually they become inert and useless to both themselves and others.

There is another group of people who go out of their way and become lost in the wilderness of the world. Neither of these extremes is good. The saying that charity begins at home does not mean that you should be selfish; rather, it means you should learn to work with your relationships in the miniature world. The family is a miniature world, and you are testing your capacity in that miniature world; that is your first training ground. Then, slowly, you expand your world from your family to your neighborhood, to your town, to your state, to your country, and finally the Center within supplies vitality to the whole of humanity. You will have many opportunities in life to do this.

We are all alive, and want to live for hundreds of years. We do not really believe that we are going to die. Nobody can believe it—I can't believe that I will die. We see other people dying, but we don't see ourselves dying. This fear of death that we acquire is terrifying to us, but we do not feel that in our daily lives. Because we are human, we have to die, so why do we not usually remember that? Actually, both realities exist: we see that people die every day, but a part of us never dies, and we also know that. If we go around preoccupied with the thought, "I will die just as my neighbor died!" then we cannot do anything useful in life, but if we understand the immortality within us, then we will be happy; then, there will be no fear.

If you really want to know how near you are to God or Reality, watch your fears and you will be able to tell. The more you live under the pressure of fear, the more you hurt yourself. The first goal is to achieve freedom from fear. Such freedom from fear is possible if you know your aim in life and that you have very little time to accomplish it. Then, you can apply all your resources to completing that mission, and no fear will come to you. But if you do not have any aim in life, then you are constantly afraid of losing things that are actually already lost. Fears are very powerful enemies.

You are afraid because you fear either losing something that you have, or not being able to gain something that you want. Whenever you have a fear, you can consider these two possibilities: either you are afraid of not gaining something, or you are afraid of losing something. By examining your fears, you can understand yourself and gain freedom from such fears.

To do this you need to take a few minutes for yourself. Many people think that meditation is the right solution, and I agree, but most people understand only one part of meditation. In meditation, you sit down quietly and repeat your mantra. During that period of meditation your mind remains one-pointed, but after that, your mind goes back again to its same previous grooves. This is not the full process of meditation; the full process of meditation is a whole life process.

"Meditation" means "to attend." It means attention to the whole of life. It should not be a strenuous act; it should not be forced. Your whole life can be one of meditation. From morning until evening you can meditate, either unconsciously or consciously, and if you do that meditation well, it will bring many benefits.

People often ask how they can do this. My method is to ask myself to consider some question that is on my mind. The source of the answers for such questions is exactly the same place as that from which the questions themselves spring. I have tried to find the answers to such questions outside myself, but once, when I was young, my Master asked me to consider where I got the question itself. When I told him that the question came from within, he replied, "Then, the answer is also there. I can give you the answer another way, but the answer is there." So from wherever the question comes, there is also an answer, and from nowhere else.

I have questions concerning the welfare of my students, because that is my life's work. Just as you are concerned about your job, so am I also concerned about my job—about my students. Those who lack hope are the first whose images come to me. There are some students who lack hope, and I think first of what is happening to them. When they come to see me I am never bothered or disturbed, because it is not necessary for me to become bothered. If I disturb myself, then I cannot help the student. If you disturb yourself about a question, you become more helpless. Your question remains a question because you cannot withdraw yourself from the conflict for some time like a second person, and watch from a distance. Instead, you identify with everything.

For example, perhaps I think someone is a very quiet person, and I want him to become a good teacher. Perhaps this question comes to me: "What shall I do with him? What shall I tell him?" When such questions that are pending in my mind come to me, I say to them, "Okay, come." I do not push them away by repeating my mantra. What *you* do, when such thoughts come, is to try to think of your mantra. This means that you try to use your mantra to avoid and escape from certain situations. Then, when you have done your mantra for a while, your mind again goes back to the same worry. That is not helpful; instead, let everything come before you for a decision—just watch.

Observe your past. Perhaps there was once a day in your past when you were in danger; you were worried or broke, and there was no one to help you. What happened to that time? It is gone; now you are here. Time is the most powerful filter. You are not the same person that you were twenty years ago; you are growing. Life is a process of growth, whether you want to grow or not. Please prepare yourself for that growth, so that it becomes comfortable for you. If you do not prepare yourself, then you remain in a state of stress and are uncomfortable, yet sometimes you have to experience even that. Your whole life is a process of growth, unfoldment, and enlightenment, but often you do not cooperate with that.

Early in the morning, right after I get up, I go to the bathroom and prepare for meditation, and then I sit down. This is the calmest period of the day, when my mind is quiet. Everyone's mind remains calm at this time. At that hour, the mind is not so external in its focus. I ask my mind what I have to do, and then I set up a dialogue with myself. You should learn to have such a dialogue with yourself. It is like a form of self-psychiatry. Self-psychiatry is one of the best things you can learn to do. Sit down quietly and ask yourself, "What do I want?"

When you do this, you will find that there are two types of desires: the simple daily wants, and the higher desires. The two types of desires are mingled together. When you sit down to meditate, you think, "I need this thing; I need that thing; I need something else! I want a good car; my car is old." These are mundane things. Do not allow yourself to suppress them by reacting, "Oh, what I am thinking! I should not think like that!" That is not helpful: instead, let the thought come before you and become a sort of observer. Start observing your own mind. Do not try to escape; do not be afraid of your thinking. If anything comes into your mind, and if you do not accept it within the mind, then it is not yours. Even your realization that a thought does not belong to you involves the thought of someone else. What is that thought that is your own thought? No thought is really yours. Try to consider a single thought that is purely yours. In all of your thoughts, there is either someone else involved or there is an image from outside.

The way to work with your intruding thoughts is to let each thought come, whether it is good or bad. Simply decide that whatever comes, you will not be disturbed. Realize that this thought, whatever it is, cannot disturb your whole life. To think otherwise means that you believe you are weak and that the thought is very powerful. What happens to most people is that any thought that comes into their mind disturbs their whole being. Then another thought comes, and that also disturbs them, and this happens continuously. Then they become weak and spineless because of such thoughts. They become afraid because some particular thought is coming into their mind. This may happen to you; thoughts that were hidden or unconscious are no longer hidden and come to your attention, and they disturb you because you react to them emotionally. You suddenly realize that a thought exists, you get upset, and then ask yourself, "Why am I thinking like this?"

The difference between you and an accomplished swami is that you take things into your heart, but a wise person doesn't take negative things into his heart. You could tell a swami, "Hey, Swami, you are a fool," and he will never take it into his heart. But you take in everything. If someone tells you that you are a fool, then you may leave and never come back, but a swami doesn't take in such negative suggestions from outside. You are constantly influenced by others' suggestions because you have not yet built your own personality. The day that you build your own personality, you will no longer be moved or influenced so easily by anyone's suggestions. Learn to build your own personality and start working on yourself.

To establish inner strength, decide that whatever negative thought occurs, or whatever others say, you will not accept it blindly. Decide that you will observe the thought or suggestion and let it come. One person may tell you that you are going to die tomorrow, and then perhaps another person tells you that you will some day become a powerful man. These two thoughts may come together: one person says one thing and the other says another. One thought is flattering to your ego, but the other thought is crippling to your willpower. Allow both kinds of thoughts to come. Be conscious of them. Whatever kind of thought comes, a thought is still only a thought. Why should you allow any thought to affect you? It will affect you only when you accept it; it will not affect you when you do not accept it. You can observe such thoughts without accepting them as your own, or letting them weaken you.

Remember the story of the Buddha and the angry woman: such people accept that which is beneficial and enlightening, and they gently reject that which is not helpful. The Buddha did not become angry or disturbed, although his disciple Ananda remained disturbed and angry for many days. The Buddha did not take in either the filth or the angry thought. That is the right attitude.

When we have crazy desires and thoughts, and we do not know how to organize them or work with them then our whole life becomes motivated by those desires. That is what we usually call "motivation," but we do not really observe or understand our deeper motivations.

Before I practice meditation, I allow all such thoughts, both "good" and "bad," to come into my mind and then go away, because they are only thoughts. There is not any thought that you can keep in your mind forever. It is not possible: a thought is that which comes into the mind and goes away. Why should a thought that merely comes and goes, determine or influence your life? Most of the time, if it is a negative thought then you feel bad. Instead, simply allow it to leave. You can control both the negative and positive thoughts that leave negative and positive imprints in your mind; let them merely come and then go away. If these thoughts are not fulfilled, they lose their power and die. This is the practice of self-psychiatry.

Perhaps a thought comes into your mind and tells you, "Come on, steal this glass." Your hand can say, "My dear thought, if you want to go, go ahead, but I am not going with you." When that happens, the thought will pass without your stealing anything. The first step is to let that thought come and pass. Even if you want to keep a thought in your mind, you cannot do it; another thought will come and will push it aside. If you think of your husband, then next, you will think of your child. Then you will think of your house, and then about your car. Many thoughts come and go; each thought is pushed away by another. There is a continuity of thought, a continuous train of thoughts. Simply let them go away.

Try to observe another thing: when some thoughts come, you begin to think about sleep. When such an experience comes, open your eyes. Do not allow yourself to go to sleep in order to shut things out or avoid things; let everything come. You merely have to allow things to come into your mind from wherever they come. Sometimes you close your eyes and sleep, so that it is not possible for you to observe the thoughts that you have stored. Then, all those thoughts come forward in the mind later.

If one particular thought comes and goes, again and again, and if you do not take any action, then it will eventually not continue to come back, because you are not paying it any interest. Those thoughts that are colored by your interest are those that motivate you to do things. Not all thoughts have that power. Not all of your thoughts need expression externally, so allow your thoughts to arise, decide if they are creative or helpful thoughts, and then express those that are useful.

The first lesson in this practice is to simply allow the thoughts to arise. Then, secondly, bring back before yourself that which is important. You can easily do this; it does not require any advanced practice of meditation. Usually, however, something important will come to you, and you either start to worry or start to enjoy your imagination. Both kinds of thoughts are actually the imagination at play during that period. Do not form the habit of merely enjoying your thinking process and indulging in it without action; such daydreaming is very dangerous. Many people do that; they enjoy and indulge in their imagination. That is not the same as creative imagination. Creative imagination is that process by which you imagine something and then, when it is helpful, allow it to be expressed through your actions.

In my practice, when all the thoughts have gone through the mind, then I sit down and start to remember my mantra. Usually you try to remember your mantra from the very beginning, and there are those thoughts waiting for your consultation, but you do not pay attention to them. Then, the thoughts are coming and going in your mind and you are trying to repeat your mantra, and the more the thoughts come, the more you repeat your mantra, and the result is an internal battle. That is not helpful; you need not do that.

If you use this technique regularly and faithfully and apply it sincerely, you will be able to really enjoy your meditation. Meditation is very important, but preparation for meditation, the cultivation of an attitude of readiness for meditation, an awareness of what you should do after meditation, and an understanding of how you should continue this meditation during the whole day, are also very important. Using this technique, you can help yourself with the four urges: food, sex, sleep, and self-preservation.

Start to work with yourself: when you work with yourself, do not waste energy observing what others are doing. Appreciate what they are doing, and do not condemn or criticize what they are not doing. Otherwise, you spend your whole life in celebrating or in mourning. What is important is that you constantly work with yourself, no matter who you are. The thought, "I am going to enlighten myself," should not make you egotistical. You should not isolate yourself; this thought should make you more creative, because withdrawing yourself from the world is not your real motive; it is not life's purpose. Your life's purpose is to live in the world and yet remain above it, and that is possible. If you decide to run away from the world, then there is nothing that you can accomplish.

A highly educated friend of mine saw how happy I was as a swami, and then he also renounced his home and became a swami, because in a way he was jealous of me. He looked at me and said, "What a happy man he is! We both used to study together at the university. This man has renounced everything and now he seems so carefree and happy!" So he renounced his family and left his home.

One day, after three or four years, we met again. We both stayed in the same cave that night. It was winter. We collected some fuel wood and made a fire. I said to him, "Let's meditate now."

But he said sadly, "I cannot meditate. All I can do is remember my beautiful home."

Thus, it is important to realize that renouncing things will not help. Action will help you, but not renunciation. If you know how to do your work skillfully, it will help you to make spiritual progress, but if you "renounce" something because you are not capable of doing it, you are afraid of it, or because you are no good at it, then that "renunciation" is not helpful. It may even create further trouble for you, because you will still remember what you have "given up."

It is better that you do your actions skillfully and not try to escape them. Lack of strength may lead you toward escapism. Then, you push things aside and say, "I'll do it tomorrow, now I will rest." Then the next day, you say, "I will do it the day after tomorrow." In this way, you keep postponing things to another day, and the day never actually comes. This creates problems in your mind. Lack of interest or fear on your part will lead to this.

If you really want to help yourself and lead a life that involves the art of living in peace, you will not try to do it by ignoring your duties. You do not have to ignore your duties to become enlightened; you do not need to change your external circumstances. External change is not needed; what you really need is the transformation of your personality.

You need to transform yourself, from morning until evening, without disturbing your duties. How do you work with yourself without disturbing your duties? If you sit down quietly for meditation but ignore your duties, you may actually hurt someone, because you have neglected that duty. Students who are not skilled on the path often do such things; they annoy or hurt others. This is an ego problem. The more you start becoming enlightened, the more gentle you are with others. Then, all things are shown to you, and all things will be known by you through your gentleness. The question is, how tolerant and gentle are you with others? Such gentleness is not a weakness; it is the greatest strength, for love is the strongest thing that you have. Tolerance, kindness, forgiveness, and love—these four make up what we call gentleness. If you are gentle, then you are very strong.

In my own practice, after I have gone through that imagery in my mind, then I sit down for meditation. My way of using the mantra is different from yours, because I do not want to fool around with the process. I sit down, and I observe my whole being listening to the mantra. I do not remember the mantra or repeat the mantra mentally, because then the mind repeats many things. Instead I make my whole being an ear to hear the mantra, and the mantra is coming from everywhere. This will not happen to you immediately in meditation, but when you have attained or accomplished something, then this will happen to you. Then, even if you do not want to do your mantra, it is not possible to avoid it. Even if you decide that you do not want to remember the mantra, it will not be possible. Finally, even the mantra does not exist; only the purpose for which you repeat the mantra is there; you are There. The mantra might still be there, but it exists as an experience that overwhelms your whole being, and is not separate from you.

To begin, you need to consider what your attitude should be: how will you work with yourself and remember that you are working with yourself? Even the worst experiences in the world can teach you something. Sometimes, however, even the best things cannot teach you because you are not ready, and you have not prepared yourself. You should work with yourselves constantly, and remember that you are working with yourself.

You should develop thirty goals for thirty days, and pick one goal for each day. Practice this yourself; it is a very simple thing. These should be small points, but things you work on steadily. For example, you may decide that today you are not going to lie. That does not mean that you will redouble your lies tomorrow, but rather, that today your whole thinking process is about this: that you are not going to lie. You never claim that you will be able to speak the total Truth, but simply decide that you are not going to consciously lie.

Then, the next day, you may resolve, "I will not be unkind to anyone," and the day that you decide to do that, everything challenging will come to you. You decide, "I will not lie," and suddenly many occasions will present themselves when you could lie. This happens because you are trying to conquer your nature, the part of your nature that you have built unconsciously for a long time. All your actions in life have unconscious results, as if you are digging a hole and therefore making a heap of dirt somewhere else, but you do not understand that. Suddenly, when you stop digging the hole, you discover that you have created both a heap and hole.

The day that you resolve, "I will love everyone and not hate anyone today," you will find that all your enemies are coming to you. They come via telephone calls, or in letters, or you may hear someone talking about you. Once, when I was young, this happened to me and I became very upset. Someone had written something very nasty to me, and my Master noticed and asked me what had happened to me. He used to tell me I was like mercury, so he called me "Thermometer." He said, "Thermometer, what has happened?"

I said, "Look at this nasty letter."

He replied, "Do you want to become more nasty yourself by replying to it in a nasty way? That is not the way to deal with it; read that letter six times, and eventually you will not find anything nasty in it." And that happened: I read, reread, and reread the letter again, and my Master told me not to reply to it immediately, so I waited, and then six days later I replied to it very calmly.

When you become accustomed to witnessing certain things in yourself, you may still feel bad, but you do not feel so very bad, and if something good happens, then you do not feel it is so incredibly good. You can develop the habit of being more balanced, of losing your destructive sensitivity and reactivity to both positive and negative things.

If you adopt thirty points to work on for thirty days, mark them on your calendar and do not tell anyone what you are doing. Just watch the calendar, and see what you have accomplished in thirty days' time. The point is *not*, for instance, whether you have lied or not lied: it is that you have built your willpower. This is the real process of building willpower. After thirty days you will conclude, "Yes, I have done what I wanted to do." But do not choose big principles that you cannot fulfill—that is destructive. Instead, select little things.

If you decide that for one day you will speak very little—only that which is accurate, purposeful, and non-hurting, you may continue to talk to everyone, but in setting this goal you will be building your willpower. After you develop willpower, you will have greater self-confidence.

When you have greater self-confidence, then you can do anything!

Lack of self-confidence is one of the points of failure in your life: you do not have confidence in yourself. For example, perhaps a husband has no confidence that his wife is going to stay with him, so he is afraid all the time. A wife may also be afraid that her husband might leave her. Some people do not get married because they are afraid they will not be happy. Lack of confidence is not something physical, it is internal. Sometimes a very physically healthy person who does not have that self-confidence can weep just like a child.

Learn to have strength from the real Source of all strength within. Willpower is essential for self-confidence. You should not be overconfident, but you should not lack confidence. Self-confidence comes after you have observed yourself, watched your capacity, and built your will. That is the way to build real personal strength. Then, you can accomplish anything.

Memory

Memory is one of the most important functions of the mind, and working to improve the memory is one part of the process of learning to use all your potentials effectively. You can benefit from the skillful use of memory—learning how to retain information. You can really develop your memory. There is an art to the development of memory, and before you can learn this art of effectively recalling things when they are sought, you need to understand the mind itself more clearly.

As we have noted, you may study books and external resources, and you may try to study the mind through books, but that is not the way. You actually need to learn to study the mind without any external help. You need to fully understand the nature of the mind itself. What do you know about your thinking process? To understand the mind and your thinking process is to understand yourself. If you do not understand your thinking process, then you don't really understand yourself at all.

The question of how your body is related to your mind and thinking process is also important to understand. The body, breath, and mind all work together. Your actions are virtually your thoughts, and your thoughts are your desires.

Those desires are mingled with your emotions, which arise from the four primitive fountains or urges: food, sex, sleep, and self-preservation. Thus, the combination of your emotional life and thinking process is what you call the mind.

As we said earlier, the mind has two separate compartments: the conscious mind and the unconscious mind. The conscious aspect of the mind is actually a very small aspect of mind, and human beings use and cultivate only this small part of the mind during the waking state in daily life. The unconscious level of the mind that dreams and sleeps you do not know much about. Why do you dream the way that you dream? Why are your pleasant dreams not repeated in the way you would like? Why do nightmares that you don't want appear in your dreams? This is a vast subject. Every individual has his or her own dreams, and you cannot compare your dreams with those of others.

You perceive things in different ways because you receive them from different angles. You have to understand that something exists between yourself and Reality, and that is the mind, your thinking process. To understand and deal with this, you have to understand clearly the different functions of the mind, which we will review briefly.

The body is like a factory, and in that factory there is a specific place where materials are imported and exported as needed. In human beings, that particular function is manas. Manas is a very important faculty in the thinking process, but what manas does is different than the function of buddhi, the intellect. Buddhi decides, discriminates, and judges, while manas only works according to the training and guidance of your intellect.

As we noted earlier, there is another faculty called ahamkara, the ego. This use of the word "ego" is different than the Western meaning of ego as being egotistical or conceited. This use of the term "ego" means the "sense-of-I-ness," or your sense of identity.

Finally there is another faculty, called chitta, the reservoir or storehouse of merits and demerits and of all memories. These four distinct faculties of mind are called the "modifications" of the mind: manas, buddhi, chitta, and ahamkara.

When a student of meditation says that he's forgotten something important, that is a very sad situation. When a student experiences that, it means that the person has never really paid attention to whatever he or she has forgotten. If you learn to really pay attention to a situation, you will not forget things. Attention and memory really mean interest. If you have an interest in something, then you never forget it. You have an interest in your home, so no matter how crazy you become or how confused you get, your feet will eventually lead you home. You don't forget your wife or children or your bank, because you have an interest in them. So when you realize that you need to search for your keys, the question is, why and how did you forget them? When this happens there is something wrong, because either you do not understand your thinking process, or you have not paid attention to things you should.

Thus, memory really indicates and reflects your interest. When you are interested in some topic, you study a book with full attention. If you are not interested in studying a subject, then it becomes difficult for you, and you cannot easily understand it. This skill depends on how you train yourself. If children are trained systematically from the very beginning, they don't become absentminded. Being absentminded means that you want to remember something, but at the same time, you don't. The desire is there, the fire is there, but you are not really giving fuel to the fire: you don't really have a full interest.

In order to develop the memory, there are a few exercises and principles you should observe. First, never criticize yourself by saying things like, "I don't remember; I know it but I don't remember it." This self-condemnation weakens you. If you know something, why shouldn't you remember it? Sometimes you can't remember something, such as the name of one of your acquaintances. The person's image is in your mind and you know the person, but you forget his or her name. There are two or three reasons for this sort of problem.

To understand this type of forgetting, you need to first consider how you perceive things. When you see something in the external world, whatever you see is received by the optic nerve, and then that impression is taken to the conscious mind, and then it is carried to the unconscious mind, the vast reservoir of impressions, memories, and samskaras. As we noted earlier, samskaras are the mental impressions of all your past experiences. They leave an imprint in the mind, and this is the process of perception.

The conscious level of the mind that you use in the waking state is only a small part of the totality of mind. Even if you are very learned or you are a genius or a great artist, when you dream, you are none of those. When you go to sleep no matter what you do with the conscious mind, still a vast part of the mind remains uncultivated, uncultured, and undefined. The unconscious is not refined or cultivated through your modern education. The vast unconscious part of the mind that remains untapped is used only by a fortunate few, by the great ones, by people such as Christ, Moses, and the Buddha. These men were enlightened and became great because they came into contact with that quality through which they learned to control the hidden part of the mind.

To fully understand memory, you need to recognize the different faculties of mind and how they function. If you have not trained the function of manas, then whenever you do something, a doubt will immediately come into your mind. This doubting function will always be there if you have not learned to channel manas. You will find that your mind constantly questions whether or not you should do something. You may want to go through a door, but then perhaps you think that you could also go through another door. Your mind may decide, for example, that when you have more time you don't want to drive to work on one route, that you prefer to go another way. Because of manas, there is always doubt in your mind, whatever you are doing.

The function of buddhi immediately decides: this way is quicker; that way is quieter. Buddhi is the function that decides; all decisions come from this source, but there is always some doubt in manas. Manas wonders if you should do something now or not, or if you should eat your meal now or a little later. Thus, for all decisions, you depend on the faculty of buddhi. Buddhi discriminates, decides, and judges.

The great sages and teachers suggest that you sharpen your faculty of decision and discrimination so that it skillfully and effectively guides your manas. Sometimes, however, you become very obstinate—although your buddhi gives you guidance, you don't want to follow it. For example, you are lying in bed early in the morning, and your buddhi knows that this is not the time to remain in bed, yet you don't get up, and thus, you form a bad habit. You know that each day you have to eat breakfast, go to the office, and that it takes some time for you to get there, but you don't get up on time. You are awake but you don't leave your bed. This is because there is a coloring of tamas, laziness or inertia in your personality. Slowly you are forming a negative habit of inertia.

The first thing that we teach apprentice swamis or serious students of meditation when they want to develop their minds is that when they wake up, they should immediately get out of bed. The number of minutes that it takes for you to get out of bed will tell you how lazy you are. Your mind will say, "Oh, it's Sunday, I don't have to work, let me stay in bed." That's a very bad way of training yourself; it's a bad way of teaching your mind. Regardless of whether it's Sunday or Monday, you should get up and get out of bed. If you remain inert in bed, you are wasting time and energy, and at the same time forming a bad habit that affects you on both physical and mental levels.

Your habit patterns weave your character; your character composes your personality, and that's who you are. The Vedanta philosophy says that ultimately we are Self-illumined, but that's not the level of yourself that I am describing here. You have a personality, and the personality has a particular character that is woven by certain habit patterns. You are responsible for your habit patterns, although your family has also contributed to that, through the way they brought you up and treated you in your childhood.

If you really want to discipline yourself and your mind and develop yourself, then the first thing that you have to learn is to get out of bed the moment you wake up, and not remain in bed tossing or turning. Rise, wash, and finish your morning ablutions, and then do something useful. Do not remain idle and inert.

This is an important secret of life: if you remain idle without doing something useful your mind thinks scattered and random thoughts, and wastes its energy. Your good thoughts should definitely be brought into action. A thought is like an unripened fruit that is not yet eaten by anyone. Ripening fruit means bringing a positive thought into action. Many good thoughts die because they are not brought into action. He who is great, successful, creative, and dynamic knows how to bring all his good and creative thoughts into action, and how to give a shape and form to his creative thinking process.

To be creative in this manner is a technique that you have to learn for yourself by forming good, sound, healthy habits, physically and mentally. A positive, dynamic person conducts his duties well and has established coordination between his thoughts, speech, and action.

There is a word in Sanskrit, "apta," which means that man who has established perfect control and equilibrium within himself. His actions are consistent with his speech; his thinking process is always coordinated. By contrast, most people start to go in one direction when they actually need to go the other, and then suddenly realize that they are headed the wrong way. This is due to a lack of training of the mind, because you have never trained yourself to concentrate and focus.

All the world's educational systems cannot help you if you do not educate yourself, but sometimes this becomes difficult. It becomes harder late in life, and as the saying goes, it's difficult to teach new tricks to an old dog. A time comes when a mature bamboo cane cannot be bent, but a young, delicate bamboo shoot can still be bent. There is always time to train yourself, but it is better to start training your children from the very beginning.

If you want to train your children, you cannot train them by words alone, because they learn more through your actions—by imitating you. Human beings cannot completely gain freedom from this habit of imitation. A child learns to walk the way her mother or father walks. You all learn through imitating. Imitation is still a prominent part of your external educational systems and that's why you are not growing. You imitate each other all the time, so you cannot create any new inventions. You do not discover something new for yourself because you are always blasted first by the suggestions you constantly receive from outside yourself.

For instance, if you ask a number of people the same question, everyone will give you a different suggestion. Everyone wants to become your teacher, but unfortunately, you have not yet become your own teacher. A real education begins when you start educating yourself and learn to discover and explore yourself without the hints or suggestions of others. A real education starts when you know yourself by understanding your thought processes, desires, emotions, and appetites.

Then, you need to discipline yourself, and you should not be afraid of the word "discipline," because to make progress, you need to train yourself. Through such training and self-discipline you can truly understand yourself. When you apply all your resources, intelligence, and understanding to exploring your interior self, the modifications of your mind, and your internal states, it is a fascinating experience.

Manas has no power to decide whether or not to do something. Buddhi, on the other hand, immediately tells you to do one thing and not another. You need to train your buddhi, the intellect, as well as the functions of manas, ahamkara, and chitta. This is the real training and the real education in life—when you start to educate yourself.

In this kind of training, books can't help you; nothing external will help you. You have to understand yourself. You need to ask yourself how you think, why you are emotional, and what the problems are with your mind. You need to question why you become emotionally disorganized, why you forget things, and why you do not attend to things properly. You need to consider why you often do not do what you really want to do. Put these questions to yourself and you'll find the answers.

First, you have to train yourself not to be the victim of sloth or inertia due to overeating or eating foods that create lethargy. Lethargy and sloth also result from not doing things on time, not forming habits which are helpful to you, or not having control over your appetites. You can regulate your habit patterns without any problems and without using any extra discipline on yourself. Those habit patterns are related to the four primitive fountains: food, sleep, sex, and self-preservation. Training the physical habits in this way has a direct result on training the mind.

Now, we will return directly to the question of how to improve your memory. If you include another five minutes in your daily practice and devote this time to developing your memory, this exercise will help you a great deal.

To develop your mind and your memory, you should first understand that whatever you do, you should learn to take a real interest in it: don't do things without a sincere interest. Doing things without genuine interest weakens and dissipates the mind and creates internal conflict. Many people do things without creating within themselves a real interest for the action. For example, some people are married but are not actually interested in the marriage. They have married, so they merely continue to do it without a sincere interest in the process. This does not mean that people should divorce their wives or husbands, but it is important to learn to create an interest and positive attitude toward the marriage or whatever you do.

If you learn to create love and interest in your marriage, then it will be successful. The key point is that without love and interest, nothing can be successful. Learning to create interest and love within yourself for something is a great education; it's a process of self-education. When marriages fall apart, it means that the partners did not learn how to create a bridge between themselves. Living means interest and attention, and living also means allowing your positive thoughts to come forth into action; that's what life means here on this platform.

The following exercise is not a meditation exercise; it is an exercise for the memory. In this exercise you don't simply begin by memorizing things—presently, your memory is blocked because you have too many things to do and you cannot handle them. When the passages between the conscious mind and the unconscious mind are blocked it is because you do not know how to handle the rush of thoughts and information coming into your conscious mind.

You have so much knowledge within but it doesn't come to your aid when you need it. You know many things, but when you need to recall something, that knowledge doesn't help you. For example, perhaps you need the keys to a cabinet and you are searching for them frantically and yelling at your children and fighting with your husband. You yell at him, "Help me find the keys!" And then you scold your child, "You have hidden the keys somewhere!"—but actually you discover that you are holding the keys in your own hand. All these actions are caused by your disorganized mind, and that is why this kind of situation occurs.

There are certain simple, easy exercises that can help you to coordinate and utilize your mind. In the modern world many men suffer from hypertension that is created by their own thinking process. In fact, of the three diseases that often cause death—strokes, heart disease, and cancer, a disease that everybody is afraid of—all three are related to the thinking process.

This is because you have two kinds of muscles: voluntary and involuntary muscles. The voluntary muscles you can contract and relax at will, but the involuntary muscles are those that are responsible for your internal organs: the heart muscle, the diaphragm, and related muscles. Many muscles are involved in these systems, but you presently have no conscious control over your involuntary muscles, because you have never learned to understand or be aware of that level of yourself.

Modern science acknowledges that eighty percent of all diseases are psychosomatic. Psychosomatic diseases originate in your mind and thinking processes, and are then reflected in your body and physical being. Unfortunately, modern science has been trying to search for the cures for these diseases in the external world. Slowly, however, modern science is coming home and seeking to understand how our thinking processes are responsible for many diseases.

There are actually very few externally-caused diseases. Most of the diseases for which we have no cures are psychosomatic diseases, created by our own minds, and by our failure to understand our thinking processes.

To begin to do the memory exercise, you need to learn a simple technique of relaxation. After completing your morning ablutions, you need to learn to consciously relax the body. Sleep doesn't actually relax you well: many times you wake up after eight hours of sleep, and yet you still feel tired. Sleep, however, can be a great medicine, a great remedy, and a great help when you are fatigued; when you cannot relax yourself consciously, then dreaming can sometimes help you.

Dreams are the expressions of those suppressions that you have stored during your conscious waking life. Certainly, sleep relaxes you, but not your total being. There is only one way to fully relax, and that is to consciously relax during the waking state. Relaxation should be a part of your daily life. Learn to relax and to reject and let go of things that hurt you.

When you consider how you love, you may understand more clearly what I mean: you actually love your enemy more than your friend, because your mind is focused on your enemy all the time. You think of your enemy frequently; you hate your enemy constantly; you are angry with your enemy all the time. So much of your energy is diverted toward your animosity—so who do you really love? You devote more time to your enemy than your lover. You want to direct your energy toward the center of your love and not toward hatred, but the opposite happens, because you do not know the method of directing that mental power and energy called "right thinking."

Nobody likes to think in this negative way. Even if you

go to a temple or a church, you may still think of your enemy. Wherever you go—even in bed with your sweetheart—you think of your enemy. How powerful your hatred is! The force of hatred in your mind is so powerful because you have never really trained yourself—you have not yet learned to direct the energy of the thinking process.

Perhaps you have learned to calm the conscious mind by not allowing the mind to run away to the external world through the agents called the senses. You gently close your eyes and create an atmosphere that is quiet: you don't hear sounds, you don't touch anything, you don't smell anything. Still, another problem arises: the mind itself is not relaxed. All the thought patterns that you have stored in the unconscious mind come forward into consciousness. Perhaps you have forgotten to do something, and you remember that you have not done it so your mind becomes tense. A relaxed mind is a mind that is not preoccupied or disturbed—a mind that remains undisturbed.

There is a time in every great man's life—a test from Providence—when he is not understood by others and may be persecuted. You may recall many examples of how great men have remained calm during these times. Socrates is one such example. When he was jailed by the authorities, his students tried to arrange a plan for his escape. But Socrates refused, because he knew that was not a good example for others. Instead, he allowed himself to be persecuted.

At the end, he joked when the cup of poison was brought to him by his jailers. He was a very humorous person and he said to the messengers who brought the hemlock poison, "Can I give a little share to my deva, to the deity whom I love, respect, and adore?"

But the messenger did not know what he meant and said, "No, it is meant only for you. You cannot share it with your deity." So Socrates smiled and drank the poison, but before he died, he said, "No poison can kill the soul."

Very few people are aware of the soul, which is not subject to change, death, or decay. You think of yourself as the mere body, because you have not clarified your thinking process. For a few minutes every day you should learn to relax yourself consciously. Relaxing by sleeping is not enough; it's much more important to learn to consciously relax. Pay attention to relaxing the muscles, the nervous system, and the mind.

There is an important difference between the nervous system, the mind, and the brain. The following analogy will help you understand: the brain is like a light bulb; the nervous system is like a network of wires; and the mind is like the electric current itself. When the electricity functions, current runs through the network of wires, if the wires are not broken. And if the light bulb is not broken, it shines when the current passes into it.

To be happy, you need to learn to coordinate these three different entities. You come to this platform for only a few moments—for a brief period. The reason why you do not attain happiness is because you forget that truth: because you do not know how to coordinate mind, brain, and nervous system!

Many people have poor memories, but this is because they have not really understood the function of memory itself. They have never learned to pay attention to things. If you truly pay attention to something, you will never forget it.

There is a great power within you: your mind is very powerful. There is nothing greater, except the Center of Consciousness within, the individual soul. The mind is second only to the soul in power, because for its functioning and expression it has the ability to borrow power from the Center of Consciousness, the individual soul.

The mind is also like a basement in some ways: you bring things home and store them in your basement and make the basement into a junkyard. Then, whenever you want to use something you remember that you have it in the basement. The mind also has many resources stored within.

The following exercise is used to improve the memory. This exercise uses numbers and will definitely help you if you do it, but most people will not do the exercise, or if they do it at all, they stop doing it before allowing it to have its effect. However, this is a very helpful and powerful exercise if you do it systematically.

To begin the exercise, sit in a comfortable and steady posture. Your sitting posture should be both comfortable and steady. A steady posture is one that puts your head, neck, and trunk in a straight line. Some sitting postures may seem to be very comfortable, but that comfort is only momentary, and the posture actually creates pain or discomfort later on. Often it's difficult for Westerners to sit comfortably in a posture on the floor, because they have not been trained to do so. If you cannot sit comfortably on the floor, don't force yourself to do so and then suffer from a pulled muscle. You can also sit on a straight-backed chair with your head, neck, and trunk erect. This is a posture called the "friendship pose," which is described in the Buddhist system of meditation.

Sit quietly and allow your body to become still and breathe deeply. Breathing evenly and deeply is the one real remedy for all stress, strain, and fatigue. Deep even breathing means that you exhale, allowing the abdominal muscles to push in, and forcing the diaphragm to move up and help exhale the used-up gases. Then, when you inhale, you allow the abdominal muscles to move out, and the diaphragm moves down, creating more space so that you can fill the lungs completely. This exercise is called diaphragmatic breathing.

Diaphragmatic breathing is your birthright. Infants breathe diaphragmatically, but because of your hectic life and the way you sleep, eat, drink, and act, the free movement of your diaphragm is upset. This becomes a habit, so you need to return to your original pattern and resume diaphragmatic breathing. If you develop the habit of diaphragmatic breathing, you'll find that you are more relaxed.

The way that you allow the diaphragm to move with the help of the abdominal muscles is a great factor in relaxation. You only need to pay attention to whether your diaphragm is functioning correctly or not. Learning to breathe in this way is a great benefit. This is how you should breathe all the time.

The next important point has to do with concentration and your mind's focus. The very basis of imagination is imagery—a form. But when there are millions of forms and images in the mind, your mind becomes confused and that creates agitation. You are trying to concentrate on a particular form, but many other forms and images disturb your mind. You need to direct your mind and focus it according to a particular system, a digital system.

At first, when you do this exercise you should observe your mental capacity, and how you memorize things. Sometimes you criticize yourself, thinking that your intellectual or mental ability is low, but you can actually expand your capacity. When you do the exercise, begin by counting from one to a hundred without saying the numbers out loud. You should count at the speed of one digit a second. You will find that it is easy for you to count up to a hundred, but when you count backwards from one hundred you may only be able to go to seventy-seven or so before you become lost, because your mind has never been trained to attend to a difficult task.

Thus, you first count from one to a hundred, and then backwards from one hundred to one. There will probably be an interruption there. You need to note the interruption and the kind of interruption that takes place. Those interruptions are very important to observe: they tell you about your mental suppressions or procrastination. For example, if you have told your wife you will do something but you have not done it, then when you do this exercise that interruption will come immediately to remind you.

When you are relaxed, your mental preoccupations come and distract you, so I encourage you not to have many preoccupations. Don't allow your mind to become congested, because whenever you relax, these preoccupations will interrupt your concentration. They interrupt your sleep and do not allow you to rest. Your mind is preoccupied with the duties that you have assumed. One day you did not have those duties, but now you have assumed them. Now, for example, you have a wife, so you should do your duty toward her faithfully. You assume duties, and each duty becomes a requirement once you have assumed it.

Learn to keep your mind free for at least a few minutes without interruption, distraction, or interference. You have never asked your mind to do this, so at first it may be somewhat difficult, but your mind will learn to follow your bidding. When you ask your hand to pick up a cup and bring it to your lips, it does so, so you should also learn to direct your mind in other ways as well. This will help you immensely.

This counting exercise is eventually extended so that you count up to a thousand and then back. When you can do that without interruption, you'll find that your mind has become very sharp. There is no doubt about the effect of this exercise. The exercise itself doesn't take much time—perhaps only ten or fifteen minutes.

As you learn to do this exercise you are learning to lead the power of mind—your thinking process and concentration—to follow a particular system, in a particular order. Thus far, the mind has never accepted any order. The mind does not want to do so, but you need to teach the mind to do that, to become orderly and organized.

You can start training your mind in this way by counting from one to one hundred and from one hundred back to one, and note how many times your mind has been disturbed while you lead your mind through the exercise. Notice also the type of interruptions that occurred, and observe the qualities of those disturbances. Consider the origins of these disturbances and in this way you will learn many things about yourself. You should do such an exercise for at least two minutes every day to retain the power of your memory. Developing a good memory means that when you want to recall something that you know, the mind will come to your aid. A good memory allows your knowledge to be recalled without any hindrance or interference.

I never teach or recommend exercises that I have not personally done. I teach only what I do and what I have done; I don't suggest exercises that are taken from books. I have done this exercise and it helped me. There was once a time in my life when I thought that I had started losing my memory, so I was taught this exercise and now my memory is perfect.

There are other exercises for the memory as well. In the chakra system you may meditate or focus your mind on a particular point. For example, you may focus your mind on the space between the two eyebrows, at the pineal gland center. This is visualized as a small circle. The mind has a tendency not to be easily focused within that circle. It never wants to be focused; it wants to move about, here and there. The ancient yogis knew that the mind resists being confined in a circle, so their technique was to bring it back to this circle again and again. In the representations of the chakras there are also triangles, which are geometrical and mathematical figures that train the mind to be orderly.

A serious student must learn to train the mind. If you have not paid this price, and have not disciplined yourself in some way or another, you'll never understand the importance of discipline. And if you allow the mind to roam and wander wherever it wants, you'll never achieve much in your meditative training.

You have to learn to direct that great force of the mind in a specific way. If you carefully observe the process, you will understand the use of either a geometrical figure or the digital counting system. If you cannot initially count and maintain concentration to a thousand, or if you have a problem with your memory, then begin with counting to one hundred.

Sometimes memory losses are due to a lack of routine in life or the way you eat. Eating healthy food is important and doing the headstand can also be very beneficial. However, if you decide to do the headstand, you should be very careful not to injure your neck. You should do the headstand only as you are taught by a qualified teacher. Many people are afraid to do the headstand. Fear of doing the headstand means that there is a great fear lurking in your heart: standing on the head symbolically means learning to stand on your own feet, and having complete control and confidence in yourself.

When those who cannot do the headstand ask about it, I tell them to begin by closing their eyes and then to mentally imagine standing on their heads. People often respond that they imagine themselves falling. Many people have no confidence in their ability to do such things. You cannot do anything efficiently if you cannot first do it mentally. If you learn to do things efficiently in your mental world, then you'll also be able to do things physically.

Working to train and discipline the mind with such simple exercises can definitely improve memory and concentration, and these are important first steps in all training of the mind.

Chapter 8

Developing Intuition and the Wisdom of Buddhi

If you want to understand intuition and the path to inner wisdom, you must first understand the avenues through which you receive knowledge. As we discussed earlier, there are three main avenues to knowledge in human beings: first, you may receive certain kinds of knowledge through your senses via the process of sense perception. When you perceive something with the senses, a process called "conceptualization" goes on inside your mind, and you form a mental concept of the object. Then, the senses continue to react and to receive and perceive information according to the concept you have already formed within the mind. You create concepts or categories that then organize other sensory experience. Thus, one method to knowledge is through the senses, but sense perception, the kind of knowledge received through the senses, is unfortunately shallow, superficial, and incomplete.

There is a second avenue or source of knowledge, and that is instinctive knowledge. You do receive knowledge through your instincts, but human beings do not remain in touch with their instincts in the same way that animals do. All the activities of animals are governed by nature, but not many of the activities of human beings are governed by

149

nature. Somehow as humans we lose that sensitivity to our instincts. You are not sensitive to nature and its subtle functions, so you do not remain in touch with instinctive knowledge.

You even lose sensitivity to a greater degree: you are not sensitive to the things around you, and that is why you have difficulty in communicating with others. You often do not understand others—you fail to understand others' language or their actions. You have difficulty in expressing yourself, and in communicating what you feel. You cannot express your knowledge or the way you think or feel through the three main avenues of mind, action or speech.

But the real knowledge in which you are interested is eternal knowledge. In the modern world, you have been trained only to understand that aspect of knowledge that is incomplete. Great poets, saints, and sages do not use the ordinary routes to knowledge, which is knowledge received through the mind and senses. For example, the great poet Tagore often said, "My knowledge is not received through the mind; it's received through a vision." Tagore would see something within first, and then that vision would inspire him and he would then act on that vision. Ordinarily, we first think, then see, and then act.

Usually, you don't see things as they are in life; you see things only partially, rather than in their totality. That's why these great people, the ancient men and women of wisdom, are called "seers"—because they knew and saw things as they are. The ancient seers saw and understood things and then they described them. They did not see things bit by bit; they saw things in their totality, as they truly are.

You will not find this level of wisdom in the process of sense perception. If you see something with your senses, you don't actually see it as it is. For example, if you merely change an object's angle, it may look quite different, and if something looks different at different times, then the description or experience of that object is incomplete and partial. When you describe something differently from time to time, it is difficult for others to understand your concept, and their conceptualization may be entirely different. Then, you experience separation from them as well.

So knowledge received or imparted through the senses is shallow and imperfect. That is why there is always doubt in your mind: "Am I right in doing this? Have I done this correctly?" You need external confirmation; you need evidence that you have done something accurately, because your sense perception is never totally correct and you cannot be secure in it.

Sages and meditation teachers say that you should meditate and sharpen your buddhi, one of the important faculties of the mind and its modifications. Why do they say that, and what is there to sharpen? There is a serious problem with human beings: if you study physics you will learn that all the things in the external world are moving. Everything is actually in motion; you are sitting somewhere and you think you are still, but you are moving. Thus, everything is constantly changing, so how can your perception be totally accurate?

There is a second serious problem as well: the mind itself is clouded. A clouded mind cannot be decisive and cannot discriminate between right and wrong. You cannot help the fact that things move in the external world, but you could at least help yourself to develop clarity of mind. If you develop clarity of mind, then no matter how fast this movement goes on in the external world, that can be recorded by the mind.

Thus, there are three reasons why you cannot record things properly with your mind and senses: one is natural to the world—that all things in the external world are fleeting and are changing fast. Another is that your instrumentation—your senses—are themselves not perfect receptors. And even if they were perfect, and there was no movement in the external world, the mind itself is clouded, so it cannot record the world clearly.

Thus, you have these three problems: a clouded mind, the limitations of your senses, and the nature of the external world. So how do you record things? How can you know things as they are? How can you end this confusion and stop these internal debates, when the senses and mind themselves cannot record things accurately? This is why you have the problems and disagreements that take place at home and elsewhere. No one actually lies; there is no such thing as a lie because no one can really lie. Even if you think that you are lying, it's not possible, because you yourself know that you are lying, so within yourself, there is no lie.

If you try to utter a sentence that is a lie, you cannot really do it. You can say unrelated or inaccurate things; you could call a table a blackboard, and someone might consider that a lie, but it is actually not a lie. It is merely that you are not relating well or accurately to these objects.

Unrelated ideas, subjects, and thoughts go on in your mind; all the time you fantasize about reality and that creates conflict for you. It is as injurious as your so-called lies. If you constantly deceive yourself, the day will come when you will no longer have confidence in yourself within; you will lose all your confidence. Then, you will need someone's advice all the time, even to confirm small things, such as whether there is a piece of bread in your hand. You will totally lose all your confidence, because you are deceiving yourself, which distorts your own mind. You know that what you are saying is not true and you are trying to say something, and that process disturbs the clarity of your mind.

Actually, no one on the earth can truly lie. If someone says something that seems untrue to you, it may be because that person is seeing something from a different angle. If you say, "Swami Rama is God," this is inaccurate; those are unrelated objects. You are not relating God properly to little Swami Rama. When you do not relate well mentally with something, then you hurt your imagination; you are trying to "tease" your imagination, and teasing your imagination will rob the purity of your conscience within. We are already confused enough, so as the ancients say, "Don't confuse yourself further by lying." "Lying" means not relating to things as you see them; it means that you are not narrating things as you see them, but that doesn't actually matter, because from another viewpoint, we are already lying, because we do not know or see things as they truly are. So no matter how much truth we think we speak, it is equivalent to a lie, because we don't yet see things as they are. Our avenues for knowledge, our instrumentation, our "employees," are not functioning according to our ultimate goal. My eyes want to see the whole, but they cannot; they have limitations. So whatever I say is equivalent to a lie, and yet I will boast that I am speaking the truth.

If you want to strengthen and clarify your mind, don't say anything that is unrelated or inaccurate. When you consciously say something inaccurate, that lie becomes something unrelated in your mind. It means that there is no communication within you then, and you knowingly disrupt your internal communication. Some people do not communicate well because they don't understand the simple principle of communication, for which knowledge is meant. Others know the principles of communication, but because of their fear, they say something unrelated or inaccurate.

When the ancient sages analyzed this problem, they asked the question, "What should we do with these instruments, our senses? Whatever knowledge we receive, we receive it through our senses. So how can we cope with this inaccuracy?" Let us now explain something about the thinking process. You wonder if your mind is more powerful than your senses. You wonder how many powers of the mind there are, and how they can be understood, controlled, and guided if you understand yourself. The sages tried first to understand the nature of their own minds.

The sages conducted internal study and research on their own minds, and their findings are explained in Vedanta psychology which describes the mind very beautifully. As you may recall, Vedanta psychology says that the mind is like a wheel with many spokes. The wheel of life within—the mind—is called the *antahkarana,* the internal instrument. *Karana* means a function taking place, and *antah* means inside: so antahkarana means your "internal functioning"—what is happening within you. That's what psychology is really trying to understand. Psychology is a science that tries to understand the science of mind, the science of your internal states. Modern psychology is also trying to explain the mind, but presently it's in a poor and pathetic state. It is only a primitive science.

Vedanta psychology explains the mind. The mind can be understood in many ways, but even if you know exactly what the mind is, you still don't have control over your mind. Mere knowledge will not give you control over your mind. Control means knowing the way in which to direct your mind. Control does not mean preventing the mind from functioning, but being aware of the mind and having a choice about the way it is directed.

Let us first consider the basic nature of the mind: the nature of the mind is simply to continue to function and to flow all the time. There is a parable in the East about the functioning of the mind. Once, there were a Queen and King. They visited an exhibition and after seeing beautiful things at the exhibition for many hours, they noticed a very small, beautifully carved box. The Queen asked, "What is in that box?" There was nothing in that one whole showroom except that small box.

The owner said, "This whole other exhibition is nothing; I have something truly great, that box is so great that no one has anything better."

The King and Queen asked again why that object was so special, and the owner opened the box and something like a genie jumped out of it!

The Queen said, "What is so great about this little genie?"

The proprietor said, "Don't call it little, Your Grace, it's great and powerful! Whatever work you give this genie, it will do it in a second's time."

The Queen replied, "We have such a large kingdom. If we had something like that, we'd be very fortunate!"

So they bought the box, and in their excitement they went home and both started working with the genie. That whole night they could not sleep: the moment they gave it some work, the genie would immediately do that work and then say, "Give me more work or I will eat you up!" They learned that they had to constantly give that genie work and keep it occupied, otherwise the genie would devour them.

The King didn't understand what to do! Whatever work they gave the genie, the genie would do it, and then say, "Give me more work or I will devour you." This became a real problem! They did not know how to handle that genie: he continually demanded more work and they were running out of things to have him do!

The Prime Minister, the wise man of the country, was finally called in and he asked, "What is the problem, Your Majesty?"

The King replied, "The problem is that we bought this genie and it is a dangerous creature. It works wonderfully; it has tremendous power, but there is something wrong somewhere, because the moment it finishes its work, it says 'Give me some more work or I will devour you'."

The Prime Minister reassured them that he'd solve the problem, and he spoke to the genie, "I am the Prime Minister of this country. I want you to get the tallest bamboo tree from the entire forest—the largest and tallest."

The genie brought it in a second's time, and the Prime Minister said, "Dig it into the ground outside," and the genie did that. Then the Prime Minister said, "Whenever I give you work, you do the work; the rest of the time you go up and down this bamboo pole." Thus, by keeping the genie occupied, their majesties the King and Queen were saved.

The great sages say that whenever you have to attend to work, the genie within your mind works, but when you want to stop, it does not allow you to rest. It functions all the time. It does impossible things; it thinks of total impossibilities. It is a magic-maker. The mind is amazing! If you think that you have imagined something incredible, just wait—someone else's mind is even more fertile and imagines something even better. The mind is a genie!

All the practices, therapies, remedies, and all the exercises whatsoever, are not really meant for the body or soul. The soul is perfect; it doesn't need any exercise or meditation. The soul needs no improvement. If you meditate, there will be no change in the Spirit. If you are perfect, the Spirit is perfect; but even if you are not, the Spirit is perfect. You need to meditate and you need help, not for the soul, but for your mind. As the great Upanishads say, "The mind is the instrument that can become either a means of liberation or a means of bondage."

Thus, you should understand the nature of your mind. It's easy to say that, but it's not so easy to actually know it. When you want to study the mind, how do you actually do it? You don't have any external device or instrument to use to study the mind, so you have to train one of the aspects of your mind to study the totality of your mind. That's another problem: there is no such instrument, there is no such power of the human being that you can apply to really study your mind. You have to train a part of the mind, so that all the functions of the mind can be studied through the use of that one part.

On this path, you yourself are a laboratory for research. Your internal states contain many instruments within you; you have to learn to use those instruments to understand the Consciousness that flows on various degrees and grades from its Center, which is already within you. Wherever you travel, your mind is there. Sometimes it even goes where you don't travel. Then you realize that you are here, but you aren't really here—you are thinking of going home! But when you are at home, you are thinking of being somewhere else—at work or on retreat. And the moment you arrive at a meditation retreat, you think of your home, your husband, your children, and your things. You are not ever here. It seems that one of the definitions of mind is, "that which is not there, wherever you are!"

There is another important concept concerning the mind: the whole of the body is in the mind, but the whole of the mind is *not* within the body. Thus, when you are trying to measure and understand your body, don't think that you can simply apply the same process and you will understand your mind. You'll fail in that endeavor: to study the body is far different than studying the mind. This should be self-evident, yet many psychologists make this mistake. In order to study the body, you can ask someone to help describe how you look. You ask your husband to tell you how you look, and he will tell you, "You look beautiful," and then you are happy.

Others can tell you something about your body, but no one can tell you, "Your mind is beautiful! You are thinking so well and pleasantly at this time." You, alone, have to observe your mind. Unfortunately, there is no training program that teaches you to do such a thing. We human beings do not know how to do it.

Our senses and our knowledge are limited to the mere name and form of the body. Any knowledge that is limited to the aspects of name and form is really very shallow, because all such forms change, and when the forms change, then the name also changes. Your whole confusion in this world lies in the fact that your knowledge is limited to forms and names which constantly change. Nobody says to an old man, "You little one, you're so cute," but there was a day when he was such a little baby. Nobody wants to kiss an old man in the same way that he was kissed when he was a child. The form changes, the name changes and our reaction changes. Once the old man was a child; another day comes, and he becomes an old man.

These constant changes take many new forms; the forms have new names and the names have new forms. We live in a world of names and forms. Our whole life is governed by names and forms, by this particular form or that particular name. If there is a particular form, we impose a name on that form, but everything changes, because everything is subject to change, death, and decay in the external world.

The sages teach that it is of no use to record these events in the external world. Yet they do not ignore the external world. They teach that one should know the secret of living in the external world. It lies in two words: adjustment and contentment. If you want to be happy at home, then adjust your behavior. You can adjust to each other. If you are stubborn and don't want to adjust, then your marriage will fall apart, but if you apply this formula, it will help you: Learn to adjust. Your other goal should not be "God" or "knowledge"—you actually need to cultivate contentment.

There is a book called the *Bhagavad Gita,* which contains the gist of the entire Upanishadic literature. It wonderfully teaches a few subtle truths, which even great scholars often do not understand. It says, "When you are a miser, you are not giving what you should give. You don't know how to give what you have. You have something, but you are not prepared to give it." If you don't know the process of giving in life, that's miserliness. A miser is he who expects to receive too many of the fruits of life without doing his actions or duties. One who expects or imagines that he will receive much without giving is a miser.

If you have not tilled your land, how do you expect the crop to grow? If you have not worked with yourself, how do you expect that highest knowledge to dawn? If you want to receive that knowledge which is the highest of all knowledge—intuition—then do not forget that no matter how many mistakes you have committed, no matter what you think about yourself, or what your friends or neighbors think about you, there is a great library of intuition within you. Deep within you, within the recesses of your being, lies the library of intuition, but you do not know how to reach it, and you don't have access to its wealth. It's as if there is wealth buried in your own home but you think that you are a pauper.

We all are rich deep within. Great artists, poets, and dynamic people unconsciously receive some of that knowledge—some small fountain from that library within, and that's why they become great. It takes very little for this to occur—just a drop of that richness. If someone receives even a drop, he starts to make poems, or he starts to paint or begins to sing or dance beautifully, because of that infinite library.

The knowledge of the mind, the senses, and instinctual knowledge, do not help in this. All those kinds of knowledge, all those resources, are important and we need them and can use them, but the highest of all knowledge is intuition. Intuition does not require any evidence at all; it does not need to ask if something is right. When you have intuition, you don't have to ask about it, because you know it's right! That knowledge helps you see things and know things as they are, and then you no longer see things incompletely and partially. Partial or limited perception can cause great problems.

There was once a man who had all the comforts in the world—a wife and children and a home. His children were grown up, so he used to attend *satsanga,* and visit swamis and yogis and listen to their discourses. Everyone talked about enlightenment and the Himalayas, and what a wonderful place the Himalayas are, so he decided, "Enlightenment is the only thing worth seeking in life."

So he told his wife, "Look, I am old now, I'm eighty. You've been a faithful wife and partner to me, and I respect you, and with all my reverence I love you, but I want to be enlightened. Will you give me permission to go? You have the children and everyone to look after you."

She replied, "I give you my permission with one condition: when you have realized something, will you come back and let me know?"

He said, "I faithfully promise it. You are my partner. I would like to impart my experience to you."

So he left and renounced his home—he renounced everything. All the neighbors and the people of the surrounding villages came to say goodbye to him. Renunciation means you don't ever come home again to claim that this home is still yours or that this wife or children are yours. You have a right to renounce if your wife permits you to, but if she doesn't permit you, then it's not renunciation; it's escaping and running away.

Renunciation means that you first have something, and then renounce it. So this man renounced his home and walked away with all his imagination, and mind undisciplined. Suddenly the man saw a ghost on the other side of the road, because such fears still existed in his mind. He had renounced his home, but he had not worked with his fears. He did not have any real knowledge or wisdom. He turned around and began walking back to his home, but he thought, "I have already renounced my family. What shall I tell my wife and children?"

A man's ego is very strong. The ego is first expressed

toward his wife, so he thought, "What shall I say to my wife? I have renounced." So once again he turned toward the Himalayas, but again he encountered the ghost. Again and again he went back and forth, hoping that eventually, perhaps, the ghost would be gone, but the ghost was still there, so he could not cross the road. Soon it was four o'clock in the morning, and it was still dark, and the ghost was still there. The ghost was just on the other side of the road, and he also saw a snake on the road, barring his path toward home.

Just then a wise man, who was also traveling on the path, came along, and he said, "Son, what's the problem?"

The man said, "Sir, I am a renunciate."

The wise man said, "I can see that you have renounced, but I don't think that you have practiced or learned anything! What's really the problem?"

And the man replied, "There is a snake on the road, and on the other side of the road there is a ghost."

So the wise man told him to come along, and gave him courage. The sage kicked at the snake and suddenly the man realized that it was only a piece of rope, and not a snake! That illusion took place because he had the habit of perceiving things merely through the use of his senses. But the senses never tell you about things as they are; they will only give you partial knowledge. When he kicked at the piece of rope he felt very foolish, because then he knew it was only a piece of rope. How foolish we are when we use only one avenue of knowledge—the senses—and we rely on them totally and suffer because of it our whole life! There are other avenues to knowledge that we should learn to use.

He said to the sage, "Okay, sir, you helped me with this problem, but how about that problem?" pointing to the ghost. The wise man told him to follow along and the man did, and when they got there, the wise man said, "That is an electric post which looks like a ghost."

Thus, mere renunciation will not make you a sage, especially if your mind remains confused and clouded. Do not forget this: leaving home does not make anyone a sage. Failing to meet your responsibilities does not make you enlightened; escaping from the world does not enlighten you either. Be wherever you are, and enlighten yourself there. You don't have to run away and go here and there. You only have to know the simplest method of working with yourself, working with all the avenues of knowledge. All that you need for perfection and enlightenment is already within you.

Why do you identify God and enlightenment with light? You talk of light: "O Lord, give me light," because light is that which dispels darkness. In darkness you do not see things properly, so seeking light means seeking to see the Reality.

The kind of knowledge that is received through the senses is very dangerous and shallow. Knowledge received through the senses is not competent, and when we act on it accordingly, that is very injurious and dangerous. Learn instead to tap those sources within which have real knowledge—knowledge that can never be challenged, that is self-evident and pure.

People don't go to expensive bars and drink the best of wines in paper cups. The most expensive wines are drunk from a goblet. To drink good wine, you need a good instrument, a good cup. To use intuitive knowledge, you need a pure body. A pure body means a healthy body and a healthy breathing process, because otherwise, they will obstruct the flow of knowledge. Why is something understood quickly by one person, although it is not understood so rapidly by another? You get confused because you accept what you see, and you don't check your perceptions. You should doubt everything—even your doubts.

Before you take action, you should confirm that what you are thinking is correct. First, doubt and don't take action until you have thought it out, and know that you are correct in your perception. If you work with yourself you will learn what kinds of thoughts are accurate and which are confused.

Those who enjoy the privilege of receiving intuitive knowledge are fortunate. The avenue of sense perception does not help to give us clarity of mind. We all know that, for none of us has clarity of mind. The input we receive all the time through the senses is so confusing that it keeps the mind clouded.

The poor mind employs those ten senses to function in the world and to receive information from the external world. Five of these are the subtle receptive senses: seeing, smelling, touching, tasting, and hearing. The other five are the gross senses, or the active senses: the hands, feet, speech, and the organs of elimination and of generation. With these senses you perform your actions. These ten senses are employed by your mind. Even if they are well trained, all the input is still filtered by these ten.

What can you do in the external world, when everything is subject to change, death, and decay? When the senses are untrained, they will give you distorted input and that creates constant confusion within. If you have accepted that there is confusion in your mind, and if you understand that, then nothing will lead you astray, but if you don't have that understanding, and if you enjoy that confusion, then your mind will create a chaos within. That confuses you even more, and there will be no end to your confusion because of this situation.

You wonder if there is any other way to create clarity of mind. You cannot change the external world, and you cannot change the nature of the senses. The instant you wake up, your mind employs your senses because they are there, and they are permanently engaged. It's not possible to avoid this situation. If you have never trained your mind in how to deal with the external world, then there is sure to be confusion. The sages teach that you should develop clarity of mind, and learn not to be distracted by the external confusion or stimulation. Sometimes you think, "When the wind stops blowing and there is no noise from next door, then I will meditate," but the noise in the external world will always remain as it is.

In some villages in India, they still use a method of drawing water from a kind of well in which a wheel is pulled by horses or bulls, and it brings up the water. The wheel makes a noise when it runs. Once a horseman came with his horse and wanted his horse to drink water. That horse was thirsty and wanted to drink, but the noise scared the horse and it would jump about. So the horseman asked the proprietor of the well, "Will you please stop this noise so my horse can drink?"

The proprietor replied, "But if this noise stops then the water will also stop." If you expect the whole world to behave nicely, and think that then you'll be able to meditate, forget it! You'll have to accept the external situation around you as it is. Accept the external world as it is. If you live near an airport, you don't notice how many airplanes are flying above, but when you first lived there, you thought it was too noisy. But there are many homes there, and people live next to the airport, and they don't hear the airplanes land or take off any more. If you learn to train your mind, then you can very easily be free from noise pollution. In order to have clarity of mind, you have to learn to train your mind.

First, you have to understand your mind, your antahkarana, and then you can think of developing clarity of mind. From the age of three I've studied with many sages, and I've thought about these subjects for a long time. I've learned about human beings from the great sages, who have devoted their time and their lives to the path of enlightenment. Through their association, by their grace, all that I have heard is stored in the bed of my unconscious.

They taught me that intuitive knowledge is the finest of all knowledge, and I have confirmed this from my own experiences. Anyone who is on the path knows it, and I am describing the same teachings to you.

You know your body, and how your body differs from other bodies. No two bodies or two faces are alike; there is always some difference, even if you are identical twins. Consider the Creator, the Engineer and Architect who created all these human beings. In each human being, all the features are in the same spot, but still everyone looks different. Consider that Artist, and how wonderful that Artist is! It's an amazing phenomena: that Providence is so highly skilled that it never repeats itself. Beauty is not repeated; it's exclusive and unique. It cannot be compared to any other, because there is nothing else like it, that particular unique individual. It means that you are the most beautiful person in the world. If you go in search of yourself, you'll never find yourself duplicated anywhere; you're the only one. Why do you not appreciate and admire your own beauty? You usually need someone to tell you that you are beautiful, but you should know it yourself. You should learn to admire and appreciate that you are beautiful, because there is no one that can be compared with you—you are unique.

So, too, is the case with your individual mind. No two individual minds can be compared, because the mind functions according to your own habit patterns. Before you express your thoughts and feelings, your habit patterns lead your mind to particular grooves, and then those grooves come forward and express themselves.

As I said earlier, your mind is like a genie. It is higher than any other power, it is faster than the speed of light or electricity; it can swiftly do things. The fastest of all entities is your mind. Nothing has ever gone beyond that speed. There is only one who has gone beyond, and he is an enlightened one. To be enlightened means to have gone beyond the speed of mind. Spirit is beyond the speed of mind. Spirit is everywhere, so the poor mind cannot match its speed. When your mind becomes aware that the Spirit is everywhere, then the mind surrenders. The mind learns that although it thought that it knew all things, Spirit is everywhere and the mind is nothing. Mind learns that all the power it has is due only to the Spirit, the Source of life, the Source and the Fountainhead of life and light within, the Source of Consciousness. Then the mind surrenders. That is the meaning of true surrender; such self-surrender is the highest of all yogas.

Your mind surrenders when you reach such a height that the mind doesn't function any longer. Mind is still there, but as it becomes aware of the Reality, its ego vanishes. It is helpful to remember the relationship between mind and ego. As you will recall, there are four different functions of the mind: the ego (ahamkara); manas, the sensory/motor mind and the thinking function; chitta, the storehouse of all knowledge, through which you receive knowledge; and buddhi, the counselor within you, and that which decides. Let us consider how this process of self-counseling happens, and how you counsel within yourself. When you do something, the faculty of manas immediately begins to function. Manas, which doubts, immediately asks, "Shall I do it or not?" The function of manas is dual: it operates both within and without. Manas is a powerful faculty; it will take in anything from outside, and it will take outside things from inside. Usually we are controlled by manas, because we do not take the advice of buddhi, the higher function. Thus, to function well, you need to coordinate the functioning of manas and buddhi.

When you fully understand these functions, you will know how to work with yourself. Suppose you want to do something: sometimes your first thought is the most accurate, clear, and useful. For other people, the first thought isn't most clear, but you should know and observe this about yourself. When something comes into your mind, do you immediately act on it? Are you motivated most wisely by your first thought, or if you think about it again, do you have a more useful second thought? Learn such things about yourself and your own mind. To do that, there is a process called "interior dialogue." In this process, you learn how to converse with yourself. You learn how you can enjoy your own company, and how to talk to yourself.

The best of all the friends in the external world or anywhere else, is your own Self. If you learn to have an internal dialogue, you'll never be afraid of yourself, and you'll also never be afraid of anyone else. Today you cannot face yourself; you don't want to know yourself because you are afraid. Once you know how to have that kind of dialogue with yourself, it will help you enormously.

Such a dialogue is itself called *upanishad*. The word *upanishad* refers to those teachings imparted by the teacher. It is a dialogue between the student and the teacher: one wants to learn, and the other wants to teach, and both are very dedicated. A special kind of loyalty and sincerity exists between them. The same principle is being applied to some degree by therapists and patients, but they are not completely honest. In the modern world, sometimes the therapist is not completely honest because he needs the income; and the patient is not honest because he doesn't want to give the therapist his money or expose his weaknesses. So that kind of dialogue sometimes doesn't really function as effectively as a sincere dialogue between teacher and student.

In this system, both the disciple and the master have that loyalty and honesty; their relationship has nothing to do with anything worldly. Whatever wealth or wisdom the teacher has, he will give it to his disciples. That is why great people say, "The burden of wisdom and truth is the heaviest. No one can carry it." The teacher has to hand it over to somebody; he will die if he goes on carrying the burden of Truth for some time. He has to give it to his students.

You may have heard the phrase, "When the student is ready, the teacher appears." There are many such sages roaming around in the world, burdened with the Truth. They are carrying Truth, and they want to pass it on, but they don't find students who are ready, so they continue to carry that burden. Fortunate are those who are enlightened, and most fortunate are those who are prepared to receive the teachings. Thus, the dialogue between the student and the teacher is called "upanishad." When a competent teacher, a great seer, has prepared his student, that dialogue is an upanishad.

You can also enter into such a dialogue with yourself, with your own inner Self, if you become a real student, and if you are committed, and have decided that you want to receive knowledge from within. But there is a procedure for doing this that you should understand. The teacher in the external world has a responsibility. That responsibility is over when he leads his student to the path of silence, from which everyone receives knowledge. Because of this, a true teacher is adored since he or she leads you on the path. The sages say that no matter how large a telescope you have, it has no capacity to see what is within you. All the external resources will fail you when you try to apply them to the development of inner wisdom. To attain inner wisdom, you'll have to abandon these external devices and learn instead to come into contact with the Truth within.

As we discussed, buddhi is that special faculty which has three qualities: it knows how to judge, how to discriminate, and how to decide. Such discrimination means the ability to distinguish between things. The deciding quality of buddhi is very important to your well-being. When you do not decide things, when you have not learned to decide matters on time, you miss an opportunity. And when you miss such an opportunity, then you regret it and blame yourself, and this damages your self-confidence. You may be very intelligent and brilliant, but if you have not learned to decide things in a timely way, you miss opportunities, and you suffer. Most of your suffering is self-created, because you have not learned to decide to do things on time. Once the opportunity has passed, then you decide on something and you wish you had taken action. That makes you even more miserable and contemptuous of yourself. Learn to discriminate and decide!

When I was very young, I spent all my time with my master and I learned everything from him. I learned from him what theft means. He never used to keep any money, but one time he knowingly kept five rupees in his pocket, and he created a circumstance in which I needed five rupees, so I put my hand into his pocket and took them out and gave them to the person who needed the rupees.

My master said to me, "Come here. You are a thief!"

I said, "What did I steal?"

He replied, "You took five rupees from my pocket."

I said, "But you're my father!"

He replied, "Of course, but a son can still steal from his father's pocket, and a father can still steal from his son's pocket."

I said, "No, I don't feel that way; that's not stealing."

He answered, "You should try to understand the real definition of things. If you train your determination, decisiveness, and judgement, then you will understand."

Then I said, "What do you mean by stealing? I did it openly, right in front of you."

He replied, "Whether you did it in front of me or not, you robbed me. You may be looking at someone, but if you rob him and go away, that doesn't mean it's a righteous thing to do!"

I said, "I still don't understand."

He told me, "You have to understand this today. Taking someone's things without his permission is theft.

Theft is when you take or deprive someone of something without his permission." And that was the last day I ever did anything like that. I never repeated that action. In your daily life, in developing your moral code, you need to understand the real meaning of things. This involves training the mind.

You also constantly commit thefts from yourself mentally, by not allowing your buddhi to function freely. If you do not allow your instrument to function, it will become rusty. And then, when you want to use it, it will not function well. You are not using the finest instrument that is deep within you—one of the finest instruments that exists—and it has become rusty with disuse, so you have to purify it. When you decide to purify your buddhi, don't allow any rust to develop, and try to remove whatever rust has developed by consciously refining your mind. That is the process of purification of the mind.

For example, the faculty of manas will say, "Do this," and it will immediately add that if you don't do that, something bad will happen. Mind will tell you various things; it will remind you that if you commit a theft, you'll regret it. Mind will teach you that if you don't commit a theft, you'll feel like a good person. It will tell you that if you commit a theft you'll become rich, but that if you are caught you will go to jail.

All these sankalpa vikalpa, these thoughts and arguments going back and forth, giving first one side and then another side of the debate—all that is the nature of the particular function called manas.

There is also another faculty which you have constantly been adoring, revering, and worshipping—the ego. You may think that you go to church and pray to God, but really you are praying to your ego, because every time you pray, you ask, "God, give me this, give me that." This means you think you are a very important person. Your "I" sense is very prominent—"I" need this, "I" need that. Your

"I" is everything to you, and God is only secondary to your ego. "I" is the word you use most in your life.

Watch how you speak all day and observe which word you use the most—it's the word "I". You have been thinking about "I" from your childhood on, so that your concept of "I" has become so strong that it has forgotten its proprietor, its real owner, the place from which the knowledge comes. It is Atman, the Center of Consciousness, that appointed this sense of "I" to its position, but the ego has forgotten its role. The ego says, "This body is mine, this home is mine, this wife is mine, these children are mine. All this thinking of "mine and thine" comes from the ego. The ego creates a very serious problem. Your ego is that which has separated you from the whole. It builds a boundary around you, and makes you petty and very selfish, and you don't want to share with anyone. The more egotistical and the more egocentric you are, the more you do not communicate with or relate well to others.

The ego is definitely helpful in many areas, providing you understand its appropriate role, but you have completely forgotten its intended role, and are feeding your ego all the time by saying, "I need this; I want this." During the whole day, only "I" is important; and all other things become secondary. Observe how much you feed your ego.

A third function is chitta, the function through which you acquire knowledge. Chitta is the storehouse of merits and demerits. Chitta, the source, the intuitive library, is within you. It will open up for you. Intuition will come like a flood. A hunch comes for a second, and then you cannot recall that hunch again. It rolls down from high above. A spark comes out of the intuitive library, and that is a hunch. The library of intuition within is chitta. When you work with yourself, then you come in touch with the finest of all knowledge, and that highest of knowledge gives you clarity of mind. Then, your whole life is a poem and a song.

You definitely have the function of manas, which asks,

"Shall I do it or not?" But if you don't have guidance, if you have not yet learned how to lead this particular part of your mind with buddhi, then you cannot make decisions on time, because you have never learned to consult buddhi. The counselor within you is buddhi, which tells you how to decide, judge, and discriminate. This process is going on inside you all the time, on different dimensions and to different degrees. You have to know yourself by first understanding your internal states; you cannot know the center hub unless you know the wheel. This wheel of the mind rotates because of its spokes, and these spokes rotate because of the hub. If you want to know the hub of your own nature, it's a very simple principle to understand.

These are the specific functions of mind, and inside, at the deepest level, there is the hub. These functions operate and these spokes rotate because of the hub, the Center of Consciousness. All power comes from the Center. The world only inspires or motivates the mind. Everyone should learn to understand their own mind. Whenever you perform any action, ask your buddhi to tell you whether it is right or wrong.

I know this will disappoint you, but it is the truth: no one outside you can give you salvation. Don't trust or depend on anyone to do that. Christ only enlightened twelve people, because the others were not yet ready. He was a great man, and he had such a great personality. He could do wonders: He could change water into wine, but He could not enlighten all the Christians. Moses could not enlighten all the Jews. Krishna could not enlighten all the Hindus. Buddha could not enlighten all the Buddhists. Mohammed could not enlighten all the Moslems. We all have prophets; we all have great religions. But, the truth is, we have to enlighten ourselves. You have to light your own lamp; nobody else will give you salvation.

The simple method to enlightenment is to first know yourself. Learn to work with yourself; don't give up in that.

Give up on anything else, but don't give up that goal. Remind yourself, "I will continue to work with myself. I *can* do it, I *will* do it, and I *must* do it." Remember these three sentences: "I *can* do it. I *will* do it, and I *must* do it."

Whenever anything comes into your mind, ask your buddhi, the counselor within, "Should I do it?" The moment you ask, "Should I do it?" it means you are counseling with your buddhi. You may commit mistakes, once, twice, or even three times, but buddhi will always guide you more and more clearly. Slowly your ego will become aware of the Truth. The day that the ego becomes aware of the Truth, that barrier that the ego creates every day will instead become a means. Then, the same power that is presently your enemy becomes your friend, and that is a delightful experience.

Chapter 9

Spirituality in
Loving Relationships

Many people unfortunately believe that to begin to walk the path of spirituality they must leave their homes and families or go away to some other place. This is not at all helpful or necessary. If you want to progress on the spiritual path, stay where you are and learn the art of living and being with your family.

You often waste time and energy in useless ways in life: in gossip, hatred of others, and in animosity or jealousy. This becomes a bad habit in your personality. In the process of transforming your personality, as we have said, your habits are very important. You should first understand your own mental habits. This is actually easy; it is not at all difficult.

In your observation and awareness in life, you normally concentrate on the externals, rather than on your own personality. Unfortunately, the first thing that you usually learn is to watch others—you watch and judge how your spouse moves, talks, and feels—you don't try to understand how or why you think, move, or speak. As a result, your entire energy becomes focused externally. All your attention becomes directed outside you, and then you do not work to eliminate your own negative habits. In the

external world, everything is subject to movement: everything is fleeting and nothing is permanent. You have to live
in such a world, and to do that well, you have to understand yourself. If you do not know yourself, you can never
know or understand others. If you want to learn about
change or self-transformation, or if you want to understand how to make corrections in yourself, don't begin by
trying to observe or correct others.

In this country, when young men and women get
married, their attitude toward marriage itself is not appropriate or helpful. You don't really understand why you
want to get married. You say that you want to help the
other person but that's not really being honest. From the
very beginning, the real purpose of marriage is not understood by either person, and thus, you do not understand
how to make the marriage successful.

Marriage is a truly great experience, an institution that
should be adored and understood, because marriage is
meant to be a center of love that radiates. But, unfortunately, in the modern world, that marriage center has
most often become a center of hatred instead. There are
two basic principles in life: the principle or "law of contraction" and the "law of expansion." You need to understand how these principles apply to the spiritual path and
to your goals in your family life.

When you speak of spirituality, you say you want to
expand your personality and consciousness, but you actually follow the principle of contraction in your attitudes
and behavior. You think of yourself only as an individual,
so you contract your personality and become increasingly
selfish. When you follow the law of expansion, however,
you learn that you are one with the universe. That realization should be your goal. If you remain only an isolated
individual to the last breath of your life, then you have not
grown—you have simply wasted your time and your life.
Then, the joy that we are meant to derive on all levels

remains only on the selfish level, and you do not ever fully understand the purpose of life, and how relationships help you to expand your personality.

According to yoga psychology, there are three qualities in human beings: the spiritual, the human, and the animal, or *sattva, rajas,* and *tamas.* The quality that establishes balance, tranquility, and equanimity in life is the sattvic quality. When you are sattvic and at peace you are serene and love all; you don't hate or feel jealousy for anyone. This is what you seek to experience.

One serious problem in society today is that people think that in order to love one person they have to hate or exclude others. In the name of love, you become possessive and then hate or fear others. This insecurity develops, increases, and makes you miserable in your day-to-day life and eventually destroys you. That is why you cannot enjoy life—because you are insecure and possessive of those you claim to love.

Life should be enjoyed without needing any external object or person. You don't need any object or person to enjoy life; learn to enjoy life as it is! First, you need to understand life—to understand how to enjoy this procession of life and how to tread the path of life without harming or hurting anyone.

Man and woman are essentially two different forces. Both man and woman can attain enlightenment, but they have not yet learned how to genuinely love each other. This is a very serious problem, which is causing society to crumble and hurting the future generation, your children, whom you expect to be good citizens.

It is you adults who hurt the children: the children are beautiful and wonderful, but their parents do not consider the effect of their selfishness on the children's welfare. Parents feel that a child is theirs, and the child should do what the parents want. Such pressure, domination, and suggestions from others do not allow children to grow naturally. You are all blasted by such suggestions about how you should be from many quarters. Everyone wants to tell you what to do, but if you analyze the person who is giving you such suggestions and advice, you will find that he or she does not really have true self-confidence. That person is just telling you what to do because of his or her ego problems and insecurity.

Your ego is a fortress that does not allow you to expand your personality and consciousness. The role of the ego should be to help you to function well in the external world, to coordinate your various activities in life, and to give direction to your mind's internal states. If you allow your ego to become dominant, however, then you cannot grow or attain anything of value spiritually or personally.

You have so little time in life, and you waste so much of it! You have to be constantly vigilant to utilize your time well, so that life becomes fruitful and useful, like a flower that blooms and gives its fragrance to all. To help you accomplish this, the family institution is wonderful.

To understand how to use and benefit from the family, you should learn the universal principle, the law of karma. As we discussed earlier, no matter what your profession or on what path you travel, you are subject to this simple but powerful law: "As you sow, so shall you reap." This law is applicable to all nations, cultures, and religions. You cannot live without performing actions in life. Even if you are a renunciate, you have to do your daily actions. And whatever actions you undertake, they always have consequences—some helpful and some negative.

The difference between the paths of renunciates and householders is that renunciates have plenty of time for practices, since they live on the charity of others, while householders have material means, but feel they have no time for spiritual practices. As householders, you are lost and distracted by earning a living, while renunciates are lost in brooding with their time.

What a human being really needs is to clearly understand life, so that life's purpose can be fulfilled and attained. This can be done if you do not scatter your energy and distract yourself. If you gather your energy, light the fire within, and bathe in that fire, then life is good. But if you scatter your energy, then your purpose in life will never be attained.

This brings us back to the question of why you marry. Man and woman expect the same thing: that the person of their dreams will come into their life one day, make them happy, and then their life's purpose will be fulfilled. Girls dream that the man of their dreams will come and marry them, but they become disappointed because they are not realistic about marriage. You have to see life and marriage from a realistic viewpoint; usually you expect too much from marriage.

From a spiritual perspective, why do you want to marry someone? Marriage does not exist for the sake of sex alone, because to experience sex alone you could go to prostitutes; there is something much more to it. Why do you really want to marry? What is that urge inside you that forces you to find someone and marry? It is that deep within, you actually want to share and to give—and that is called love.

This word "love" is the least understood and most misused of all words in the modern world. People tell their partners they love them but they don't really mean it, and they lie to the other person. If you love someone you don't lie to them—that's not love! You know only one kind of language, and that is wounding someone's heart and mind by suggesting to them in person that they look beautiful, and then when they're gone, you resent them and criticize them to others.

There is no reason for people to live like that. Both men and women express their resentment and anger at their partner, but feel that there's nothing they can do—

what's done is done. With that kind of attitude you live together under the same roof, nagging and being nagged your whole life, and all your energy in this relationship is wasted. It would be better for you to establish understanding and a bridge between each other.

Sometimes men and women think that in marriage they will become one with their partner, but that's not possible. Don't try to do that; for two to become one in that way is not possible. Instead, you should become like an eleven, with two separate and independent numbers. If two people consider themselves to be like an eleven, then they will enjoy this life together, because each is respected as an individual. It is important to learn to respect each other personally. As an individual you should respect the other person's independence. If you have this attitude to begin with, then try to understand the other even more fully, and add to that respect and love.

Love is learning; love is learning to maintain respect for each other. Love is not that spontaneous thing you feel for someone that is merely sensual. That feeling is not love; it dies in only a few days' time. Love is understanding; it is giving. When you love, you give and give and don't expect anything in return. When you learn to give and you understand that the real law of life is giving, and that the more you give, the more you receive, then you will know that love is giving sincerely, not expecting things from the other person all the time. Your expectations are the mother of all your problems in life: you expect too much from each other. Both women and men fantasize about relationships, expect too much of them, and are then disappointed. Once you realize this, you can adjust your expectations and create harmony in the relationship.

I once lectured at a conference in Germany that five hundred prominent psychologists attended. They invited me to speak, so I said, "If you allow me to say the truth, I will come." I asked the audience how many of them were divorced, and eighty-five percent of the therapists were divorced. Then I told them they were responsible for the crumbling and disintegration of society. I wanted to confront them: if counselors are divorced, and believe that divorce is better than learning to adjust to each other, then how can they help people remain married?

Such people often counsel others but sometimes they don't really try to understand and help the couple. For example, they may suggest that the couple separate for some time and live apart, and sometimes the partners think that psychologists are the modern gurus, so whatever they say must be right. People pay counselors to help them improve the marriage, but the therapists tell them to separate, and the patients don't know that this counselor is only projecting his or her own inner feelings and conflicts onto the process.

This is a recent trend: if two people come with great hope and pay money to receive help, the therapist may say they should separate for some time and see how they feel. That's not a cure for the problem! Therapists should not make a living by encouraging such things; they should learn to create bridges and better understandings between partners. Where couples are not communicating, they should try to help them to communicate more effectively. If the therapist does this, then counseling is a good and helpful profession.

Teachers, doctors, psychologists, and counselors should be responsible for their actions. They should try to counsel and assist their patients so that misunderstandings are eliminated. They should teach people to understand each other again, and reestablish communication, so that family life is not destroyed. Otherwise, the children suffer most.

In your society, the teachers and guides have themselves become irresponsible, so your children do not learn the important things. Children do not learn through language and books, but through example. When a child sees what his parents do at home, the child misbehaves or lies. The father or mother gets angry and spanks the child, so the child is bewildered, "My mother and father lie, so why am I not supposed to lie?"

Family life is the ground for training children. The day that you understand that you have not come to this world merely to fulfill your own selfish motivations, but to serve others, that will be a great day for you. The word "service" in Sanskrit is *seva,* which also means "to enjoy." To serve others is not a process of merely obliging others, but you should actually enjoy the act. The finest of all acts is to give without any strings or attachments. If you do give sincerely and lovingly and then observe the results, you will realize that the best deeds you have done are those in which you gave without strings or attachments.

To learn to give lovingly, you need to work on your habit formation. So far, you've formed the habit of being selfish and you see only your own viewpoint and desires. You need to learn to give to others and not to expect any reward from love. You receive the rewards of love when you are no longer in the world.

Love means to give unconditionally, and the mother is a symbol of that kind of love, because of how she experiences a pain like death when she gives birth to a child. A mother does that out of love. She can deny herself anything; a good mother does everything for her child.

If you really love someone it's not that difficult to adjust to each other when you decide to marry. But it is better not to marry than to get married and then become divorced—to hurt someone or to be hurt by someone. I have observed and collected data on marriages throughout the world, and I have learned that arranged marriages have often been more successful than these modern so-called "love marriages." When you "love" each other, you show only your best parts to each other; this sort of love does not lead you anywhere; it's based only on superficiality.

Marriage is something powerful, sacred, and wise. If you accept somebody, and if you are accepted by somebody, you should learn to understand that person, adjust to them, and give to them selflessly. Learn to understand that person; don't try to destroy someone's personality. Learn to understand, adjust, and give unconditionally.

All married people should observe one law: at home you should learn to give to each other without any conditions or limitations. Outside the home, protect yourself first, and then act, but at home, you should rely totally on your partner and do not protect yourself; act spontaneously. Great and gentle people who are wise will never allow their family life to be disturbed. Don't allow anyone to disturb your family life, because your family is meant to be a temple of peace. When you are tired you can rush home to your wife and children and find solace there.

There are many couples who lead very successful, prosperous, and busy lives, but who do not know how to have a close dialogue with their partner and do not discuss things or communicate fully. For them, many important things in life remain unspoken and are not understood. They do not learn to expand their personalities and communicate.

People fight because they don't understand each other. Learn to discuss things with your partner; all problems can be solved and resolved if you discuss them. When you discuss things, don't become stubborn or domineering, with the attitude that because the person is your wife or husband, they have to listen to you. Don't forget that you are two separate and individual lines. There should be a sense of equality between you.

One of the great Persian poets said, "On the ladder of love, the first rung is reverence." The moment you lose respect for your partner, there is something wrong with *you*. The moment you feel a lack of respect for your wife or husband, your love is gone. The word *bhakti* means love plus reverence, to have both reverence and love for the other person. Learn to give with reverence, and then there will be no conflict between you. Respect does not just "go away"; if it is gone, try to establish it again and again. If misunderstandings rob the purity of your reverence from your heart and mind, then work to reestablish it.

In all situations, learn to discuss things and to communicate. Sometimes it doesn't matter if you even call your partner names; this is letting out your feelings, and it can sometimes be therapeutic, if it does not go beyond that. You should allow others to let out their anger or frustration, and you should learn to receive it. You should have the understanding that when the other person is angry you will not speak or argue. Then you will really understand each other. If you allow the other person to let out his anger, then after a few minutes he will say, "I'm sorry," and you can resolve the problem. Learn to have patience with each other.

Once I met a couple, and the woman was as beautiful as a statue, but her husband loved someone else, although they had two children. I wondered how the other woman could be superior to such a beautiful woman. The man respected his wife, but he did not love her.

I said to the husband, "Your wife is most beautiful! Everyone in the whole country thinks you have the most beautiful wife!" and he suddenly began crying. I asked, "Does she love you?"

He said, "I don't think so, but my girlfriend does." I told him I wanted to see his girlfriend, and the next day I went to see the girlfriend, who was actually an ugly woman. I couldn't understand what was wrong, because he preferred his ugly girlfriend to his beautiful wife, so I asked him, "What is the matter?"

And he said, "Swami, what do you know of married life?"

Happiness in married life has nothing to do with the

attractiveness of faces, dresses, or such things. These last for only a few days, months, or years. That which is really important and beautiful in human beings is their behavior. The best part of a human being, that which can be enjoyed most, is his or her behavior—the way they talk, walk, act, and gesture—that is real beauty. Real beauty lies in the person's behavior.

The *Bhagavad Gita* says, "The person of attainment, the enlightened person—how does he walk, how does he sit, how does he think?" A human being can be understood and known by his or her behavior, actions, and speech. Those who have coordinated their thinking, speech, and actions so that they are harmonious are truly beautiful.

The superficial concept of so-called beauty is fleeting and does not last forever. What is important is behavior, and right behavior is learned by children in the home, when parents behave well and teach their children to communicate positively with others. Children learn by example, so if the parents do not set a good example, then the children will grow up with problems in how they relate to others. If you behave badly toward your partner, you are not only harming your partner, but you are also harming your children, the future generation of the world, whom you expect to convert this world into a Garden of Eden.

Religions usually pay attention toward three aspects of behavior—good speech, thoughts, and actions. Good thoughts are those which are not negative, passive, or selfish. Good action is that which is meant to help others selflessly, and from which you do not benefit personally, but you spontaneously do the right action to help others. That is the real concept of beauty. Real beauty lies in these three things: your actions, thoughts, and speech.

How do you allow your good thoughts to be brought into action? You would like to be good but you cannot, because you have not been taught how. You don't understand the real value in life: that the principle of life is giving; that's the only way to liberation. There is no other way; you can pray for a hundred years, become a great swami, and prosper, but if you do not understand this law, you are doomed. The law teaches you to go on doing your actions skillfully, selflessly, and lovingly.

When you understand life from this very practical, down-to-earth viewpoint, then you see things as they are. Presently you don't really want to see things accurately because you are wearing colored glasses. When you see things as they are, you will see that the external world always changes, but there is only one entity that is not subject to change—the Center of Consciousness. We live in a world of change, yet we should be aware of that Center of Consciousness—that's the practice of spirituality in the world.

If you really love your partner, then you should not love or respect only the body and your partner's skills. You should love him or her because you see God shining through that face. There is a Light in that lamp. You love the Light. You don't love the wick, the oil, or the stand. You love the lamp for the sake of the Light. You should establish the same awareness when you get married and establish a home—love the Light in your partner. If you do not establish this awareness, it is because you are selfish.

Selfishness is trying to hold on to things in life to control or possess them. If you try to hold on to the water while you are swimming, you will drown. The principle of swimming is to push the water away, to give and not to hold on. In life you also need to renounce and give. If you understand this law it will make you very happy: learn to give.

Who does not want to give to others? Only one who is insecure. You want to get married because you are insecure; you cannot live without somebody and that is why you want to marry someone; it's a simple thing. You also want to get married to be fulfilled. Your Light needs acknowledgement; you should also acknowledge the Light in someone else. You are Light and he is Light, and the Light is only One. Then why is there a problem? The problem lies in understanding: you create a barrier between you and Reality. If you want to learn the art of loving, learn to give. If you have learned to give, then you know you are already liberated—and liberation comes.

You are bound by a self-created bondage, a bondage that is not created by God, so praying to God cannot help you. Why should you pray?—you suffer because of your own actions. There is, however, one good reason to pray: because when you pray, you gain energy, courage, zeal, and strength from within. That's the real reason for prayer.

Prayer can help you, but prayer alone is not the answer for learning to work with your actions. You have to deal with your own actions, for you are the owner and master of those actions. Prayer helps in other ways, but not in the area of your actions. When you realize that you have committed a mistake, simply do not repeat it and then you are free; you are forgiven by yourself. If you have forgiven yourself, then the Lord has forgiven you. Usually, however, you have guilt feelings because you haven't forgiven yourself, and when you don't forgive yourself, then you project your anger and negative feelings onto your partner and make her life miserable.

This whole family institution, this world, is created by woman. Even buildings are the idea of woman. There are many male architects, but they have actually learned architecture from woman. Men were irresponsible: they used to live in caves, under trees, and underground. They did not know how to build a home. Woman taught them this. The idea of home is a woman's idea; when she became pregnant, she wanted a shelter and things for the children.

Tagore expresses something about woman in beautiful and poetic language: "O woman, you are half woman and half beautiful dream. Let me live in that dream eternally with you. O Lord, give me that dream again and again so that I love my woman to the last breath of my life."

Learning to love your partner is wonderful and it's an adjustment. When you understand that, then you have to do your actions skillfully and lovingly. What does loving action mean? You do certain actions and then you think you are a great karma yogi; so you earn and become a good provider, or you feed your children and look after your wife and then you think you are a great, spiritually advanced person. That's not enough! You should learn to do your duty with love—*that* is something great and profound. When you do your duties with real love, *then* you have learned something.

If you do your duties mechanically, then you are no more advanced than the clock Big Ben, giving time to the world, but not knowing that you are a timegiver. You should do your actions, but do them lovingly. Learn to create this attitude in your mind. If you do something for your wife, such as getting her a cup of tea or a glass of water when she's not well, then bring it to her with love. If you just bring water and dump it on the table, then you are doing the action, but there is no loving duty. All your actions should be greased with love.

I don't understand how you can live without loving people. If you cannot love one person, how can you love the whole universe? And if you cannot love the universe, then what is the use of talking about God? The part of your behavior that is important is how loving you are. It is also important that you learn to understand your own behavior and your mind, action, and speech in a positive way. It is important that you learn to communicate with your partner and discuss things. Don't keep brooding on thoughts or feelings inside yourself. When you do that you can't understand each other, because you don't discuss these important things.

Weak moments come in everyone's life when there is a gap in communication. When you do not communicate with your own husband or wife, it means the problem lies with *you* and not with the other. But both partners should think that way, they should learn to discuss things. Never leave things undiscussed; then your communication is broken. Communication does not begin on the physical level or through speech or letters. Real communication starts on the thought level.

Learn to express your feelings and thoughts to your partner. Learn to understand each other; make your life beautiful. Time is short, the work is vast, and we have to cross this mire of delusion; it cannot be done by being all alone.

You are all lonely because you have made many experiments, but you have not attained or established real spirituality—that is why you are lonely. Spirituality alone can make you happy. The human frame will not make you happy. You are together to attain something and that is spirituality. Then you are fulfilled and you'll no longer be lonely. Everyone is lonely. You are lonely because you have not attained your goal, and your goal is to acknowledge the Reality and the Lord in your partner. If you cannot love your one person, how can you claim to love God? How do you claim to love the universe or the cosmos? To begin the process, learn to be loving to your husband or wife. Set aside a time to talk to each other, let out your feelings in a creative way, and enjoy life. That is the true path of spirituality in family life.

Learning to Be
Your Own Therapist

I have been questioning myself and asking others also some difficult questions that no one could answer for me: what is therapy and why do you need therapy? What are the therapeutic agents, and who is your therapist?

To put these questions in perspective you should first understand something about life. The body is subject to change, death, and decay, but the soul is immortal. This is a fact accepted all over the world by all the great cultures. For example, when Christ was at the Sea of Galilee, he told his disciples that the body perishes and the soul is immortal. If this is true, then where lies the problem? Once you understand that the body perishes and the soul is immortal, then where is the trouble? The trouble lies in our mind—that which stands between the body and the soul. An entire sadhana with many practices is devoted to the mind. We may speak generally about this concept of "mind," but every individual has an individual mind. To truly understand the mind you have to understand your own thinking process, and not only your thoughts, but also your emotions.

Let us consider the emotions and how the emotions arise. Perhaps you know that you should be nice to your wife, and be gentle, kind, and loving to her, yet you suddenly become emotional, and you yell or hit her, which you never meant to do. If you continue doing that, you are sick, and if you are sick, you need therapy.

Therapy means the process of learning how to be normal and balanced. To attain that normalcy, you need a kind of therapeutic understanding. If you ask how one becomes normal, there are several important points which you need to understand. If you work with yourself on these points you will benefit, and your therapist will be amazed to see how much progress you have made. All therapists and teachers should teach their students and patients these four things: how to regulate the four primitive fountains which are the very basis of all problems   the desires for food, sex, sleep, and the urge for self-preservation.

First of all, many problems arise because of the issue of food and how we manage our need for food. If you eat imbalanced and unhealthy food, you will soon become emotionally imbalanced, because you are not supplying the necessary nutrients to your body. Ask those who suffer from diabetes how depressed they are: for them, there is nothing good in life. Thus, you can analyze emotional disease and discover its relationship to food. If you do not supply the proper diet to your body, your body will demand it. You supply a bad diet to your body because of your bad habits, because of the appetites that you have acquired. There is no such thing as a natural taste or craving for these foods. That kind of appetite is something acquired and created by the cultures of the world. All the cultures of the world are considered to be great by their inhabitants, but I do not think they are so great; all cultures are primitive. We human beings are primitive. No one tastes the food as it is. Certainly, you should cook and bake food, but unless you put in spices or ingredients that have no nutrients, you do not want to eat food. No one eats food as it is, in pure form; you eat food because of your acquired tastes. Thus, we acquire certain food and appetite habits which are not healthy. This is the influence of our culture. We do not eat good and healthy food; we do not supply our bodies with that kind of food which is needed by the body and which the body demands. Instead, we feed the body junk food and this results in many problems.

A second primitive fountain is sleep. I did research on the anatomy of sleep at our laboratory in Hamburg University. One day, I was one of the participants, and I decided to see what happened when sleep came, and then I could not sleep, because I was watching my mind and as long as I watched my mind, I could not rest.

Sometimes you can become too fussy in trying to understand the mind. The mind cannot be understood by the mind itself; it is not possible to understand mind through the mind. There is something beyond mind, but "beyond mind" does not mean that it cannot be reached. Beyond does not mean far away or unattainable. This is wrongly translated; according to Vedantic philosophy and yoga philosophy, "beyond" means within. Your senses are beyond your body, your mind is beyond your senses, your soul is beyond your mind. Beyond means inside, at a deeper level; do not search for that which is beyond on a superficial level. When you become conscious of something within you that is beyond the mind, when you depend on that which is deeper and finer, instead of depending on the mind, then you can understand the mind. You often think that the mind is omnipresent; you listen to the dictates and whims of your mind and follow them. If you continue in this manner, it will take you several lifetimes to understand mind.

You can try to use a tape recorder and record everything you think: millions and trillions of thoughts pass through your mind in just half an hour's thinking. If you try to record them all, it will take you a day. One day's thinking will take you a week to record. In this manner you can see that the mind is not easily studied. This is the external way of studying the mind—what modern science is trying to do, and that's why it is a failure. That's why the aspects of psychology are not accepted as scientific. There are two different concepts; one is doing an experiment in the external way, and the other involves doing experiments within. That latter system, which leads you to the deeper levels of your being, is an entirely different system. In internal research, you don't have any external means to help you; you have to help yourself. You have to understand the system and how to go about studying it. You have to understand how to be within yourself systematically. Just as you try to form certain systems, codes, and disciplines for research in the external world, so do you also need a method for research in the internal world, but to completely understand the mind is not possible.

The external world constantly confuses the mind because everything in the external world is moving and changing. Physics says that all things move, and when something is constantly moving, then the mind is clouded, and it cannot accurately record the event. You cannot stop movement in the external world; that's a fact. You can do only one thing: you can have clarity of mind. How do you attain that clarity of mind? To develop clarity of mind means to establish an understanding between the major functions of the mind.

Mind itself has four main functions. Manas, which you call sensory/motor mind; buddhi, which you call intellect; the aspect of ahamkara, is called ego, and the aspect called chitta, through which the entire knowledge flows, your storehouse of memories. When you understand these four functions clearly, then you understand that every function is important. Even when you understand all the separate functions, you have to understand one problem: your mind wants you to do something but your intellect refuses.

This happens frequently in your daily life: your mind

says you do not want to work today, but your intellect tells you that if you do not go to work, you will not get paid, and you will not be able to pay your bills. So you are going to work against your mind and your own attitudes. On the other hand, many times you go with your mind and don't follow your intellect. In this way, there is a constant division within you. That constant division creates a conflict, and such conflict within and without is the source of all illnesses, physical and emotional. Nobody outside yourself creates illnesses for you. It is your ignorance of your physical and mental habits that makes you ill. The more difficult part of yourself to work with is your habit patterns.

Now, let us analyze what happens with habits: anything that you do repeatedly for a long time becomes a part of your life, and that is a habit. When you try to analyze your life, consider all your habits; they make a mask for you, and that is your outer shell, your external life. You all are beautiful from within, because the soul is immortal—everyone has that. But, you consider yourself to be bad and you condemn yourself because of your emotional habit patterns, which have created a mask for you. Your habits have made your personality for you. Your personality—whatever you express, whatever you understand, as far as you can go—is made up of your habit patterns, and all your habit patterns depend on the four primitive fountains.

Understanding one single emotion is not going to help you much. If you consider an emotional problem, for example: "I become emotional and angry with my husband. He comes home tired and I should not do that." Even if you can stop that one behavior, there is still something at the root of the behavior that you do not understand. Somewhere, there is an imbalance in how you manage your primitive fountains—in food, sleep, sex, or self-preservation. Many years ago, "Mama" was the first chairman of the Institute in Chicago, and she was a very loving person. We had a wonderful relationship. The first time she came to see me she was suffering from arthritis; two people brought her to see me in Chicago. I looked at her and suddenly something came out of my mouth; I said heartily, "You are my mother—how is it possible for you to be crippled and need to be supported by two people." I told them to leave her alone, and said to her "Walk to me!" She walked over to me, and both the people were surprised. I told her, "You are my mother, and you are going to be all right." She hugged me and cried, and we became like a mother and son. But she had a bad habit: she was really overweight. I said, "Mama, you should lose weight, you know."

She said, "My diet is fully controlled." Her sister Kitty said, "She eats everything in the refrigerator and she doesn't allow me to eat it, but she doesn't remember that in the morning." Why did she do that? In her sleep, she would go to the refrigerator, eat, and go back to sleep, and in the morning, she would scold Kitty for eating the food. One day I sent one of the Institute girls there to discover the real situation. I told her not to say anything, but to simply watch. That night, the girl found Mama going to the refrigerator for pie. So I told the girl to remove all the pies from the refrigerator. The next night, there was no pie when Mama opened the refrigerator door. Then she opened her eyes, she found herself at the refrigerator, and realized that she had been doing it.

Many things that you do, you do unconsciously, although not necessarily in sleep. You are not aware of what you do or why. When you do something unconsciously, it means that your habit pattern is very deep, and you are not aware of it. When you do things unconsciously it means that you accept a kind of helplessness in that area, and when you have accepted defeat, that's the worst thing you can do to yourself. When you accept defeat in working with yourself then you secretly condemn yourself, and then, when someone else says something you resent, you become outraged and offended.

When you lie and then condemn yourself, you lose your willpower and your power of determination. In doing so, you hurt yourself, so then what can your therapist do to help you? He or she cannot observe such internal things. If you lie to other people, they will tell you, but if you are lying to yourself, then nobody can help you. Even a good person can do that; even a very good person, a gentle person, who has been helpful and loving to others, may constantly lie to herself or himself. To avoid this, you have to understand the levels within yourself. To understand your unconscious mind, you have to be alert and observant and work with yourself gradually. Do not be harsh to yourself: the mind is like a river and you cannot stop its thinking. Mind is like a river, and if you try to create a kind of dam or reservoir in it for some time, and become like a beaver, trying to stop the flow of the river, eventually there will be a great disaster. Therefore, do not try to stop or suppress your thinking. That's a bad way to try to understand or control your mind.

There are two ways to work with your mind. The first is that you can learn to introspect, which means "inspection within." To do this, sit down and observe what you are thinking. You actually already know; you really know all your weaknesses, and actually you are busy hiding them, so if you go to a therapist, but what can he or she do? The therapist cannot help you because you are hiding from yourself. In therapy, you try to become very truthful; both parties must base the therapy on honesty. Unfortunately, that doesn't always happen and that is why therapy does not always help. Sometimes you hear of someone who has seen a therapist for fifteen years, but nothing is happening. Sometimes patients become so dependent on their therapists that they will not move or make decisions without them. That level of dependence on others hurts you.

Depending too much on either a therapist or a teacher is not a good thing. They exist to help you become healthy, happy, and self-reliant. If you are not becoming self-reliant, healthy, and happy, then leave your guru or your therapist. Either he is not helping you or you are not following the advice of your therapist.

The principle of communication begins on the thought level, long before you express yourself in letters or words. You and I have been communicating long before you even thought of reading a book or I thought of writing or lecturing. Communication between two people starts even without their knowing it, without their seeing each other. Communication originates from the thinking level, and then you express yourself externally, through your speech or actions.

Let us continue the subject of working with the urges: unless you have regulated your primitive fountains, your therapy will not work. In saying this, I am being blunt, and perhaps I am disappointing or offending you by saying this, but it is true. I am not saying that you should not do sex, nor am I telling you not to eat, I am merely telling you to begin to regulate the time at which you do these acts. Whatever you eat, the right kind of diet should be supplied to the body. Those who want to lose weight will find it is really very easy. To be overweight means that you are overeating, so the first question is, why do you overeat? This often happens because you are not supplying a proper diet to the body. Your body is demanding food because something is missing and so you gain weight. If you supply the proper diet to your body, you don't need to try to lose weight in any way; your weight will be in accordance with your body. You gain weight because you are not supplying the proper diet. Try to understand the nature of the body and your dietary system.

The second question is, why did Mama go to the refrigerator and eat like that? She was never married, and was from an Irish family. I knew the cause of the problem, but, at the age of 79, where would she find a boyfriend or a husband? There is a principle of compensation in the human body. That principle of compensation means, for example, that if something is wrong with your pineal gland center, so that it is not functioning properly, then your pituitary gland center will take over. The pituitary will function, but it will have to do double work. If someone can see with only one eye, it is a strain on that eye, because it has to take over the work of the other eye. The principle of compensation serves in emergencies, but if the pituitary gland is forced to go on functioning that way for a long time, then it also stops functioning from overwork. Because Mama never had a sexual outlet, she used to overeat. Many people overeat because they are not sexually happy; that is one of the reasons for people getting fat.

The sexual urge does not start through the body. Sexuality starts in the mind. Food is a necessity of the body first, and then of the mind. Sex is a necessity of mind first, and then is expressed through the body. Those who are sexually compulsive or obsessive have something wrong on the mental/emotional level. There is something wrong with their habit patterns or there is an ego problem. This problem can be analyzed and understood. If you regulate your diet and the rest of the primitive fountains, then you can become your own therapist. You are learning something from your internal therapist; you are learning to discipline yourself and do things at the right time.

Once I went to a Police Station to observe criminals, because the Deputy Inspector General was my disciple. I wanted to understand about the habit patterns of criminals, so when he interrogated criminals I went, but I didn't dress like a swami. I wore a suit, and went in and sat down quietly. Twelve convicts were imprisoned there, and he asked them, "You have been in jail four, five, or six times, so why are you here again?"

One said, "Sir, I know what I did is a bad thing. My crime is not a good thing; I don't like it, but, I am helpless. I have formed a habit and I just want to do it."

Another said, "I don't know what else to do. I only know how to steal. It's my habit. If I learn how to do anything better, perhaps I will not steal."

The third said, "I love to trick people! The truth is I love to trick people and I like to see how intelligent I am. I want to see how much I can steal from others, but I have not yet perfected the art, because I get arrested."

Everybody gave a different sort of explanation, but finally it all came down to one answer, and that is their habits. Habits can lead you either to jail or to heaven. That is why the *Upanishads* say, *"Manayiva manushyanam kara nama bhanda moksha ho."* It is mind that creates hell and heaven for you. These two concepts exist in the mind. Heaven is a concept of tranquility; hell is a concept of great distress. It is the mind that creates both. You have glorious opportunities to create heaven for yourself.

Don't hanker for other's approval or worry about what the world thinks of you: that can become a great complex. Many people behave very nicely but only because they worry about what others will think. That is not good; when you act that way, it means that you have become subject to something external and have become a puppet. What you feel you want to do from within, if you go on doing it and are committing a mistake, you can correct. But what you do only because others want you to do, you can never correct. You should learn to do what you feel. Learn why you feel as you do and what you like. Why do you like something? If you go on learning and understanding, finally you will learn what is right for you. That which is not wrong is always right.

You will understand this point more clearly in this way: the sense of self-preservation is the highest fountain in us. We seek to protect ourselves all of the time. Consider a reflex action: if I throw something at you, you protect your head with your arms. That's a reflex action. All the time you are afraid; fear is a major part of your life. In your entire life, your major motivation is fear, yet you never try to examine your fears. You should sit down and ask your mind what your fears are. If you do that, you'll discover that all your fears are imaginary—all are the result of your imagination.

Your imagination is an image within, but you receive that imagination from outside. There is actually no fear inside you. If you experience fear, you have accepted some image from outside and put it into your mind, and then you hold it, love it, think of it, and become part of it, and that is the imagination—that is what you are doing to yourself! Then, you condemn yourself for your fears. Why should you condemn yourself? Throw away that imagination and you are free. Don't allow your mind to condemn yourself.

Sometimes you know you have done something that you think was bad, but that doesn't mean *you're* bad. That's merely a deed; it's an action. How can you come out of the influence of this regret? You should simply not do the action again, and then you are free—your mind is free. You will not reap the fruits of your actions because you are not doing the act. If you are mentally free, you are physically free.

The first type of freedom is mental freedom from fears and guilt. You constantly experience guilt. How can you improve that? How can you attain the goal of your life if you go on experiencing guilt?

Do not identify yourself with your past deeds. When you do that, you think, "I did this act the day before yesterday, so I am a bad person." If you think this way, you will not improve. Ramakrishna Paramahansa says, "If you go on thinking that you are bad, bad, bad, then you are bad. Then, you can never improve. You will have to come out of the influences of your past impressions, which you carry in your heart and in your unconscious mind."

When you do wrong, and you do not know what you are doing, then you are forgiven. But when you knowingly do something, you are not forgiven and you will reap the consequences. The consequences come through your habit patterns; but you can discipline yourself. Gradually and slowly, you can work with yourself; don't give up. Finally, you'll reach the summit, and you'll attain what you want. If you think you are too weak, go to someone who is stronger and he or she will help you.

Another important question is how to deal with the sleep urge. There are two types of sleep. One is the sleep that makes you unconscious, that which you think of as sleep. But that unconscious sleep is not really very healthy. Just as eating junk food unconsciously is not healthy, so, too, is unconscious sleep not very healthy. It helps in one regard, but not in the deepest way, because even in unconscious sleep a part of the mind still remains awake. Perhaps you are sleeping and suddenly somebody touches your body; even though you are asleep you will brush their hand away, because some level of your mind is still alert.

Thus, even when you go into a state of deep sleep, a part of the mind remains unrested. What are you going to do with that aspect of mind? You never learn to work with it or develop it; that's why you need to do meditation—to learn relaxation, so that you can consciously give rest to that part of the mind which is never rested. That is why I tell you to meditate. It's important to do that.

There is also a type of conscious sleep you can learn that is called "sleepless sleep." The sages say that a fool goes to sleep, and comes out a fool, but if a fool goes into meditation he comes out a sage. That's the difference—a fool goes into meditation, and he changes—he comes out a sage. Meditation is a conscious habit, while sleep is unconscious. Meditation gives complete rest to both conscious and unconscious mind, while sleep gives rest to only one part of the mind—the conscious mind and not the unconscious part. Meditation is important in order to provide complete rest for your body and mind.

Real meditation has no brand name—there is no distinction between Hindu meditation or Christian meditation. The world is tuned in to such foolish ideas. Meditation should be therapeutic and systematic. You are a human being and you have a body; no matter where you are, you should learn to rest. You should learn to have a healthy body, and you should learn to calm your mind. You should learn to relax your mind. You should learn to breathe properly. That will provide rest to the important system of the your body called the involuntary nervous system. If you do not do that, then you will have much more trouble with stress-related diseases.

Diseases are constantly increasing and the number of hospitals are increasing. Everybody is a patient. This is happening all over the world. Perhaps with one problem, you can be helped by a therapist. If you have formed a bad habit of developing many problems again and again, no therapist can ever help you. Your best therapy is to learn to understand "self-therapeutic" values. Good communication begins when you first learn to communicate within yourself. When you are your own best friend, then you are the friend of all. As long as you are your own enemy, don't expect the world to be your friend. Then, everyone seems to be bad, and everyone seems to be looking at you in a suspicious way, because that's what you think about yourself. The day you approve of yourself and fully accept yourself, on that same day, the world will finally accept you. Just as your face is an index of your heart, your heart is an index of your soul. The way you feel and the way you think is the way that you act. You can help yourself.

Learn that method of self-therapy which is comprehensive, and which truly helps you. Learn that method that tells you not what to do or what not to do, but *how* to do it. Within yourself, you have a lab for experimentation, and you can work with yourself. Don't accept the idea that you are bad or weak or incomplete. You are a human being. This imposition of the idea that you are bad or good is due to your habits.

People say that they condemn themselves. My response is, "Who are you to condemn yourself? Do you belong to yourself or do you belong to God?" If you belong to God, then what right do you have to condemn yourself? You have no right to condemn yourself; you have every right to criticize your actions. Your actions are yours, but you belong to God, so you don't have the right to condemn yourself.

If you study the basic laws of human life, you'll understand that a human being is always pure and simple. In the areas where he needs training and therapy, some of his habit patterns are deep. These patterns are deep because of his childhood: certain seeds are sown in childhood and become part of our life, and that's why we think something is right and something else is wrong—we develop such convictions. But at the same time, whatever we receive from our ancestors, we also receive something harmful from our environment—bad habits which are injurious.

If you go to an Indian restaurant, your palate will start watering because of the spices. You order and you discover that your mouth is watering. This is a bad habit. Or perhaps you go to Italian restaurant and so you automatically think, "I should have some good wine." These are just habit patterns, and habit patterns can be modified. They can be changed, and then you have achieved something. Presently, you have not attained anything because you have already attained a state of mind that is enveloped by dust. If you simply shake off the dust, your mind is clean. All efforts can be made and you should make a sincere human effort. Even if you make only a fifty percent human effort, then another fifty percent of the power will dawn, and that is grace. Human effort brings about grace.

Why is one person "graced" and another not? Because he has made a sincere human effort. Why does one human being go into samadhi? Because when he says, "O, Lord, I have honestly done all that I can, there's nothing I can do beyond this, through this body," and then immediately grace dawns.

When you have made your human effort, help comes from above. That is the "descending force." When you have used all your own ascending force, then the descending force of grace comes. Let God grace you and bless you.

Sometimes in the morning you will realize that you have not slept well. This is a very simple thing: in the morning you feel tired and lazy. On days that you are fully rested, you don't feel that way. Sometimes your sleep is robbed or disrupted by some unconscious agony, some thought or fear. The day that that happens, you'll be tired, but the day you have fully rested will be different. It is better for you to sleep after doing a little bit of relaxation and breathing. Then you'll have a complete rest.

The five most important conditions and requirements for therapy are first, honesty; secondly, selflessness; next, understanding; the fourth trait is the ability to watch the progress. The goal of leading the client toward self-reliance is the fifth requirement. These five conditions are very important in any therapeutic process.

If you send a person to see me for five minutes of counseling, when the person comes out, he will be smiling. If you send the same person to another therapist, when the person leaves, he goes out crying. This is because the therapist's pocket comes first. I want the client to feel good, to feel nice and gentle. If the therapist's economic needs become secondary, then therapy works.

When you have done all your actions skillfully and

selflessly, you gracefully reap the fruits of your actions. You enjoy the act, because there is grace in it. You make your own grace. You supply your own grace. There are four types of grace; the grace of guru, the grace of the scriptures, and the grace of God are the first three. However, these three help you only if you have your own grace. If you don't have your own grace, then these three do not help at all. These three depend on your own grace. When you learn to enjoy the fruits of your actions gracefully, then you are graced by God. The grace of God is light. The sun is there, the moon is there, and all the lights of the world are there. This is grace. But you don't have the grace of your own self, because you have made your eyes blind-folded. The moment you obtain your own grace, this grace of God is there as well.

Chapter 11

Parenthood
and the Spiritual Path

If there is ever any real profound and peaceful "revolution" in the world, it will take place within the family. When the human being fully understands life, he will not create revolution on the streets, damaging and destroying things in the external world. The real revolution will begin from the home.

How do we create a good home? How do we have healthy children? How do we create that kind of discipline that is healthy for children? Once we know this we can change the whole world: we can take another step in the development of civilization. We have done enough research on mind, matter, and energy. If we decide today that we really want a good and healthy society and we decide we want to change our society, we can change the entire society in thirty or forty years. But to do that, we will have to change ourselves and our habits, so that we have healthy children, and so that the children learn from the very beginning to love and share. It is possible to achieve this.

All over the world man has been very selfish and cruel, and it's a pity that man has not given full opportunity and rights to woman. Woman is the creator of our society and

207

all over the world that you see around you, she's the first architect of culture. When she became pregnant, she wanted a shelter and a home. A woman is definitely superior to man, but I am not talking about those women who are irresponsible or selfish. I am talking about those women who are women, who understand. Women have been exploited for many things. But if there is anything that can change the course of humanity, it is woman. The day that woman understands who she is, and the immense power that she has, she will transform the world in a short time.

Woman is being exploited in the world, but she should be respected, revered, and loved. I think the time has come when we are becoming aware of this. Man and woman are equal partners.

Whether you are a man or a woman, if you want to develop spiritually, you should never be afraid of responsibility. Modern people are afraid of the word "responsibility," but responsibility is not something bad. Responsibility is learning to give only the best that you have. The word actually means the ability to respond. In responding you give of yourself. A teacher or parent should always give the best that he has. It is something you should learn to do naturally as a child; you should not learn to be afraid of giving.

By nature, children are very selfish; they do not have an awareness of others' existence or needs, but if children are taught to give from their early childhood, then giving becomes a part of their life and they learn to take joy in giving. Then, a child's growth is not stunted. The mother is the first teacher of the child, and if she does not impart the right knowledge to the child, then the child does not really grow or mature well. If the mother does not know how to give lovingly and freely to the child, then the child becomes selfish; that child does not know how to live.

Those who are irresponsible are actually very selfish. Selfish people become even more irresponsible. But the more self*less* you become, the more you will find that you have a kind of freedom that cannot be imagined by your mere mind. In the modern world, you learn to live only for yourself, and you learn to use the things that you have or want to acquire for yourself. This is one concept or approach to living. But if you understand that you are meant for others, and you want to serve others and live for others, that is an entirely different way of living. The first concept contracts your personality; the other concept expands your personality—that is the difference!

When you become selfish, you create boundaries around yourself and live in a self-created imaginary fortress. When you become selfless, then you expand your personality, because you don't think of yourself alone. Many people do not communicate well with others or trust others because they were not taught to give. That is why a great poet said, "Give me only the first seven years of my life, and the rest you can take." The best and most important period of life is childhood, and if the right seeds are sown in childhood, then one truly grows and develops.

Certainly everyone grows up, but often you grow up in a wild and selfish way. If you are trained correctly, then you will learn to give. One of the great educators of the world said, "A child is trained twenty-two years before he is born." This means that the child is really educated when the mother is trained.

When a mother has a child, she should be attentive and careful to impart the subtle lessons that help the child grow. The reason why there is so much disharmony in our society is that children are not properly brought up or taught to give. You are taught only to judge things and to accept others' values—to think that one thing is good and another is bad.

In the modern world, the main responsibilities of a human being are not usually imparted in childhood. That is why you remain irresponsible and selfish throughout life.

The role of the parent or teacher is to teach you to be unselfish. Your first teacher was not the person who taught you philosophy or yoga; it was actually your mother. If the mother was a bad teacher, then there is always a cross to bear in life or an obstacle to overcome in your growth: then throughout your life you don't trust anyone.

In childhood you learn through imitation and example; you don't learn through books, mere words or through culture or philosophy. You learn by seeing what others do. When a mother and father are good examples for the child, then that child is very happy and secure and he or she grows up without fears or selfishness. That is why modern society is still in a primitive state: it has not yet attained the height of a culture where you truly learn to give to your children. So these days, although human beings are growing, it happens in a wild and selfish way.

When you give, you have to sacrifice. That kind of sacrifice is higher and more difficult than the mere idea of giving. Those who want to have children and those who are already parents should learn to give up their selfishness and give their children the kind of knowledge that is helpful and healthy for them, so that they can, in turn, impart the same knowledge to their own children.

When the time is right, then the next step comes: an environmental education where you learn from others' behavioral patterns and from how others around you behave and feel. You develop empathy. Then, if someone cries, your heart also cries. You could be cruel and hate that person if you have learned that, but to be like that is not really a natural phenomenon; it is not the natural response. If the child grows up in an atmosphere that is not healthy, how do you expect that child to become a good citizen, and to help others?

Historically, man is not the first teacher of the child; the mother is the first teacher. The father's influence comes second. If the early training is not adequate, later on, the person's whole problem comes to the attention of the spiritual teacher, the *acharya*. He has to deal with all the student's negative thoughts and habit patterns. If the mother has completed her responsibilities, and the father has completed his duties, then helping the student becomes the acharya's job, and it is not difficult. But if the parents have not done their work, it becomes very hard for the student to change and develop. The teacher tells you to come to him, but you go in the opposite direction because you have become very resistant, stubborn, and negative. You don't accept things as they are. You accept things only if they are as you *want* them to be. That is a very serious problem in your learning. To learn to "let go" is an important part of childhood training. Those who are fortunate have received that training. A child does not merely need simple or tender care, but the parent should also carefully observe how the child's personality is growing and developing.

Responsibility really lies with women. Woman is the true builder of the world, not man. Man has always been irresponsible, but now in our modern world, woman has also become irresponsible, so there is chaos in society.

In the modern world, we have many means and opportunities, but we do not know how to use those means. We have explored many avenues and alternatives in the external world, but we do not know how to use those opportunities well or *why* to use them. This is a very serious problem in modern life. As a child, your mother and father should teach you to walk and move in a straight, comfortable, and balanced way. They should teach you to speak in a balanced and pleasant way, and to interact pleasantly with others. And when you have learned those basic things, then the acharya or teacher explains to you the "why" of life; he answers the questions, why are we alive and how should we live?

Years ago, when I went to the Soviet Union, I asked

the Russians some philosophical questions: "Why do you eat? Why do you aspire to have good food and a good living?" but they couldn't really give me a good philosophical answer. There should be a purpose in your life; the purpose of a good life is so that you can conveniently attain your natural needs, and then you can more easily explore the higher stages of life. If you have many obstacles and difficulties, it is hard to explore the higher steps. All the things in the external world—making a good income, having a good home, and owning things that are helpful to you—are all intended to be means. But if they are not understood and used as means, then they can create obstacles. The same things that can become means to a higher goal, can also create obstacles for you. In the family, a good husband or wife who helps you and shares with you is a means for your comfortable living, but this relationship can also create serious problems for you. Your problem is not with the means of the world, it is with the way you use them.

To help a child grow, a parent should have inner strength, and that inner strength lies in compassion. No one can love anyone in the way that I was loved by my Master. A thousand fathers and a hundred million mothers couldn't have given me that kind of love, and because of that I never missed my parents. Even today I don't miss my parents, because of the way I was looked after and the love I was given.

You can tell whether someone is phoney or genuine when they say they love you. Most often, you do not know what you really mean by the word, "love." Real love is when you do things for someone and do not expect anything in return—that is the nature of genuine love. But how do we learn such love? We mostly learn through the examples of others' behavior and not what they say. For example, there was once a father who visited prostitutes, and unfortunately he and his son visited the same prostitute, but neither of them knew that the other went. One day they met there. The father was shocked to see his son, and he became angry and said, "What are you doing here?" The son became arrogant and said, "The same thing that you are doing here!" And the father replied, "Do as I say, don't do what I do."

This is the problem: you expect your children or students to learn what you say, but they actually learn what you *do*. You always want the best for your children; you don't want them to pick up your bad habits. You know what your bad habits are: what is bad in you is what is unhealthy in you. You may not want to admit this to yourself, but you know it. Your bad habits are your arrogance, your egotism or your selfishness—but actually, all these traits can be summed up in one word—selfishness.

You should certainly know *when* to give and *how* to give. But first, you should create the zeal and desire to learn to give. To instill that, the parent should have compassion. Compassion means that you love your children, and you want your children to grow, learn, understand, and practice. That attitude should exist in the parent.

Sometimes wisdom flows through you. When you have compassion, all good things will come through you. If you don't have compassion and if you are selfish, then only the negative will come out of you. When you are learning to teach your children, your first responsibility is to develop compassion for them. You can do wonders with the help of compassion, but if compassion is not there, then imparting knowledge is like planting seeds in a barren field in which nothing will grow. Thus, the first stage of a parent's growth is to develop compassion.

This is why yoga science teaches ahimsa, which means non-violence. If you want to practice non-violence, you must first know what it really means. Love comes before truth; satya (or truth) is developed later on, but first, you have to understand ahimsa. You cannot practice truth if you do not understand ahimsa. In developing love or ahimsa, the field of your practice is where you live—with your family, friends, colleagues or your neighbors.

Your goal is to practice truth and love and learn to speak the truth. Your parents told you to speak the truth and to love others, but their teachings don't explain how to do this: you need to have an example of love and truth. All the great bibles and scriptures of all of the cultures in the world say you should love others and speak the truth. But how do we love others?

Yoga science teaches that if you want to develop love, then you should first do no violence. Whether you are learning to love your husband, wife, children or friends, the first thing is to do no violence in action, speech or mind. If you have refrained from hurting, injuring or killing, then you will naturally come to love. By observing this principle of ahimsa, you are loving and practicing truth.

As a parent, this means not to allow any selfish feeling in your heart toward your children, expecting that your child will give you something. You have to prepare your children for your teaching. Preparing children to learn is more important than imparting the teaching. When you learn how to prepare your children, you teach them basic things. Their foundation is very important; if a solid foundation is not there, then a castle cannot be built. If a castle is built on sand without the right foundation, it cannot stand. The foundation may seem primary, but it is very important, and the first cornerstone of that foundation is your compassion.

There is one single characteristic that has existed in all the great people of the different traditions in the world, and that is selflessness. Christ, the Buddha, and Krishna all attained the highest wisdom, but they remained themselves. Your outer individual shell will remain exactly the same, but your inner light will expand and expand to universal Consciousness. That individual flame of love will become a forest conflagration and will burn up the precarious weed of your selfishness. Selfishness is not needed; it will get in your way. Truth will automatically come to you if you learn how to love. Don't approach love in a merely external or superficial way; offering your body to somebody is not love, it is merely lust. I am talking of that kind of love in which you are completely selfless. In such love, you want to give and you feel great joy in giving, and you feel that this is something great for you to do as a human being. You need to learn to give and truly love, and compassion is the first step.

While you are learning to teach your children, you should also have another goal: you should develop an enthusiasm about learning from your children too—children are also teachers for their parents. You can learn many things from your children; often the parent doesn't have the intense desire to learn that a child has. You should learn to keep that zeal alive. Never close the gates of learning; they should remain open. There is no end to knowledge; don't allow yourself to think that you know everything. Always remember that you still have more to learn, because there is no end to your learning. This knowledge is *ananta,* limitless. With such a love, you teach your children and attend to each child personally.

Set a time for your practices, because that is how you develop habit patterns and teach your children to do so. If you are used to eating lunch at one o'clock, you will feel hungry at one o'clock, no matter where you are, even without a clock. If you have developed the habit of waking up at five o'clock in the morning, your eyes will suddenly open at five o'clock, even if you are tired. It is helpful to form a habit of doing your exercises, breathing practices, eating your meals, and going to bed at exactly the same time every day. These are four important functions that you should regulate. You will enjoy life better if you do this.

Actually, all four of your appetites should be controlled. When you learn to regulate all your drives, that is real human development. When you are married, you know you have a spouse and do not go with another partner. This is part of what is meant by regulation of the sexual urge. You should also regulate the temporal aspect of your behavior—the times in which you do things. Don't just decide to have sex the moment that you come home—learn to prepare yourselves for the experience. Sometimes a woman does not feel prepared for what her husband wants. Sexual desire does not originate in the body; it originates in the mind, and is then expressed through the body. Sexual desire has nothing to do with virility or strength; it has something to do with emotions and the way you channel and express your emotions. It is better to have an understanding of your partner and his or her feelings so that you are not disappointed in your expectations of the relationship.

You should also regulate your food intake and teach your children to do so. If you eat regularly at the same time, it helps the system to function. Your sleep schedule should also be regulated. Yogis reduce the amount of sleep to two and a half hours, and finally to no sleep. They call it "sleepless sleep," and they go to a state of deep meditation instead of sleep. When meditation becomes your whole life then this change naturally occurs.

In a healthy lifestyle, you should have time for exercise, breathing practices, and meditation. You should also understand that you were born and anything that is born is sure to die. Brooding on death and creating fear is not a helpful thing to do. Sooner or later everything changes and everything dies. You will lose only your body, which dies and decays. Why should you be afraid? Again and again you need to remind your mind of this, because you have not been taught to do so; you have been taught to look after yourself fearfully. People said, "Don't go here, you will fall. Don't go there, you will have an accident. Don't go here, someone will kill you." All those kinds of negative suggestions are stored in your mind, and thus, you become afraid. Most of the fears in your mind are imaginary. You analyze many things in your life, but because of your fears, you never analyze your own fears.

When you go to a teacher, you want to get rid of your fears. You explain them to him, and he gives you strength and inspires you. But the teacher can only inspire you. It is your responsibility to see that your children improve, progress, and remain fearless and happy. Even if you live for only five days, if you live those days cheerfully and fearlessly, they are wonderful. If you live miserably for five hundred years, then those five hundred years are of no use. If you want to live for a long time, learn to be cheerful. But aspiring to live for a long time without doing something creative or useful in life is of no use. Don't give up and say, "O Lord, take me away." You only do that when you feel good for nothing. You have worth and value; you can do wonders for others. The more you act selflessly, the more inner strength you will develop. When you have inner strength, you will become free of physical pain. The body may experience pain, but you will not feel it. Then, the time will come when you will not be affected when the garment of the body is snatched from you.

Slowly you should learn to be an "insider." An "insider" is aware and attentive to the Reality within. An "outsider" is only aware of the external reality. Don't remain an outsider throughout your entire life. Make gradual progress: at first, you may only be an insider twenty percent of the time and eighty percent an outsider. Slowly, when you go within, you will grow to become fifty percent an insider and fifty percent an outsider. This is a wonderful combination, because you are half there and half here. Before the light of the body extinguishes, learn to focus all your awareness within. Then, you merely leave your shell here. In this way, you will make gradual progress.

I encourage parents to practice ahimsa. This requires strength; love is inner strength. Love alone is the only real strength. The sages live in the forest and they have no weapons to protect them, but they remain safe, because they practice nonviolence to such a degree that even the most violent animal becomes calm in their presence.

I had that experience once with a swami near Rishikesh, where there is a temple called Chandakali, in a deep forest. There was a swami who lived there in a thatched hut, and the whole forest around there was full of tigers.

One evening I went to see him at eleven o'clock, and he said, "How did you come here all alone? It is very dangerous to travel at this hour of the night. You should go back now!"

I exclaimed, "You just said it is dangerous to travel now, but you are sending me back into danger again?"

So he half-heartedly allowed me to remain and sit down. He was baking a large bread in a *dhooni,* a kind of fire, and the loaf was rising and swelling. I asked, "What is this huge bread? It is big enough to feed twenty people! It is huge!"

He said quietly, "My kids eat a lot."

I was surprised and asked him where his kids were and if he was married, and he answered, "Yes," but there was no cottage around.

Suddenly I heard a roar: Tigers! He said to me, "One of my kids has come now," and the tiger came and sat down near there. I didn't see the tigers but my whole body suddenly shivered and shook, and I thought, "I am finished now!" The swami said to me, "Be quiet, please," and he broke the bread in half and asked the tiger, "What happened to the other kid?" And then the tiger and its mate came and sat down near him and looked at him, and the swami gave them the two huge pieces of bread. Then he clapped his hands and said, "Go now," and the tigers left. He said, "I tamed them, you know. I live here alone; sometimes I felt lonely so I started talking to the animals. It is possible to do that." I have even known of people who tamed wild elephants with love.

There is a way to tell how much love you have for others: sit down quietly and calmly examine your fears, and see how much fear you have. The more fear you have, then the less love you have. If you have less fear, then you will have more love. If you have no fear, you are able to give complete love. Your fear will tell you how much love you are capable of. Learn to live in love and not in fear. Always be cheerful, compassionate, and giving. Let Providence work and trust that you will receive what you need.

There is nothing that is really yours. You become attached to things and people, and then you think that they are yours, but they never belong to you. Things are meant for you to use, but they are not yours, so don't allow yourself to become attached to them. Things will always disappoint you. Unauthorized ownership leads to misery. Enjoy all the things of the world as long as you have them, but don't become sad the moment they are gone. This should be your attitude in daily life.

If you always remember two things you'll never be sorry. These two things are death and God. Death will help you realize that you eventually have to leave here, that this world is only a platform, and you are merely on a journey. Remembering God will help you realize that you are strong; He is within you. Wherever you are walking, you are walking with Him. God is with you, so you are strong. Death is there to remind you that this physical self will finally go away, and not to become attached to the world. You have only to complete your duties and your responsibilities.

You often wonder how you know what your duties are. Whatever you do and wherever you are, pay attention to the things that are occurring in the present—that is your duty! Whatever comes in front of you is your duty. Understanding this is important to both students and to parents.

Chapter 12

Understanding the Process of Meditation

Many aspirants misunderstand meditation. They think it is a practice of withdrawing from the world, of avoiding one's responsibilities and one's relationships. Meditation is not needed for this; you already have many ways in which you avoid and withdraw from your duties and responsibilities. You live with fears, concerns, strain, and struggle, and because of your preoccupations, you are not responsive to the moment, you are not fully present and aware. Furthermore, your inner and outer conflicts interfere with your ability to deal effectively with the situations that come before you. They prevent you from relating harmoniously with those who are close to you, and from accomplishing the tasks that you have placed before yourself.

Meditation is a practice of gently freeing yourself from the worries that gnaw at you, so that you can be free and responsive to the needs of the moment, and so that you can experience the joy of being fully present. Meditation is not what you think, for it is beyond thinking. You do not meditate on your problems in order to solve them, but through meditation, you see through the problems you have set up for yourself.

Meditation is a simple and exact procedure of becoming

aware of who you are. It is learning to know yourself as you really are. All of your training has been to know the outer world, and to become skillful in manipulating the external world for your apparent benefit. However, unless you learn to know yourself, whatever you do in the external world will be insufficient and will not produce the results you want. If a tire is out of balance, no matter how wonderfully it was designed in other respects, no matter how much research went into compositing the material, or designing the tread, it will not function properly. Unless you achieve inner balance, no matter how much you know about performing in the outer world, you will fall short. Meditation is the means of achieving this inner balance.

When a meditator probes the inner levels of his being, exploring the unknown dimensions of interior life, he needs to learn a systematic and scientific method that can lead him to the next state of experience. Then, he can go beyond all the levels of his unconscious mind and establish himself in his essential nature.

From childhood onward, we are taught to examine and understand things in the external world, but nobody teaches us to look within and understand the mind and its various states. After examining the objects of the external world, a human being finds that he has not yet understood and known himself or his internal states. Anyone who has examined the objects of the external world and their transitory nature understands that life has more to give, and then he starts searching within himself, and conducting "inner research." To do research in the interior world, we have to apply an exact science if we really want to know the Center of Consciousness hidden deep in the inner recesses of our being. Many students turn toward meditation out of curiosity or excitement, and try to understand themselves and know their internal states. Some of these students persist and others give up exploring their inner dimensions.

All the existing spiritual traditions of the world use a syllable, a sound, a word or set of words called a *mantra* as a bridge to cross the mire of delusion and go to the other shore of life. *Mantra setu* is that practice which helps the meditator make the mind one-pointed and inward, and then finally leads to the Center of Consciousness, the deep recesses of eternal silence where peace, happiness, and bliss reside.

Unfortunately, many spiritual traditions have somehow, somewhere lost this science of mantra. They remain scratching the surface of spiritual experiences, muttering a few words which they call prayer. Prayer definitely purifies the way of the soul, but the method of meditation is a systematized way of exploring the interior self and the inner states of human life. There is a vast difference between prayer and meditation. Prayer is a petition to someone with a particular desire to be fulfilled, while the method of meditation leads one from his gross self to the subtlemost Self. Those who are students of life can clearly understand the difference between prayer and meditation. Prayer, meditation, and contemplation are different tools and different ways for attaining the goal of life. It is clear that the method of meditation is not a ritual belonging to any particular religion, culture or group.

The meditative tradition does not oppose any religion or culture, but teaches one to systematically explore the inner dimensions. Some Westerners are uncomfortable with the word meditation, and think that meditation is an Eastern tradition, forgetting that the Bible clearly says, "Be still and know that I am God." Learning how to be still is the method of meditation. Meditation is beneficial for physical, mental, and spiritual health.

In meditation, the first thing one has to learn is to be still. The process begins with physical stillness. The student is guided by a competent teacher to keep his head, neck, and trunk straight. According to the tradition that we follow, the *asana,* or the meditative posture, is carefully selected according to the nature and capacity of the student. A good student selects a sitting posture and learns to become accomplished in it. After accomplishing stillness with the help of the meditative posture, the student becomes aware of obstacles arising from muscle twitching, tremors occurring in various parts of the body, shaking, and itching.

These obstacles arise from lack of discipline, because the body has never been trained to be still. We are trained to move in the external world faster and faster, but nobody trains us to remain still and serene. To learn this stillness, a regular habit should be developed and, to form this habit, one should learn to be regular and punctual in practicing the same posture, at the same time and at the same place, until the body's habits stop rebelling against the discipline given to it. This primary step, though very basic, is very important, and should not be ignored. Otherwise, the student will not be able to reap the desired fruits of meditation and his efforts will be wasted.

Contemplation and meditation are also two different methods. Meditation is a specific method, and it is like a ladder with many rungs which finally leads to the roof, from which one can see the vast horizon all around. Contemplation also uses a systematic method to examine the principles of life and the universe, constantly assimilating these ideas and transforming the whole personality. Those who are fully dedicated and have given their whole life to the goal of self-realization use both methods—meditation in deep silence and contemplation in daily life. Contemplation is seeking and searching for truth, and meditation is practicing and experiencing truth. The Lord of life is truth. Learn to practice truth with mind, action, and speech. Secondly, love is the Light of lights. Learn to radiate this love by not hurting, harming or injuring others. Contemplation is practicing and applying such ideas in daily life.

All the great religions have come from one and the same Reality. Without knowing the absolute Truth, the purpose of life cannot be accomplished. Though the schools of meditation and contemplation are two different schools, they can both help a student go beyond and establish himself in his essential nature. Our essential nature is peace, happiness, and bliss. It is the mind that stands as a wall between apparent reality and absolute Reality. Mantra is a means, meditation is a method, and the constant state of awareness of absolute Truth is the attainment which fulfills the purpose of life.

Meditation has nothing to do with beliefs. Thus, it is not allied to any religion whatsoever. It is a practical means for calming yourself, letting go of your biases and seeing what is, in an open and clear way. It is a way of training the mind so that you are not distracted and caught up in its endless meandering. If you meditate regularly you will find that you have become more calm, yet alert to what is needed at the time. Most people associate calmness with passivity, but the equanimity that meditation brings frees up your energy so that you can apply yourself more fully to whatever you undertake. Worry and preoccupation dissipate your energy, while meditation releases the energy that has been bound in your mental discord, so that the energy is at your disposal. Meditation will lead your mind to become more concentrated, so that you can fully focus on whatever you choose. Because of this increased ability to concentrate, a person who meditates will learn almost anything more easily and more quickly.

Meditation will also lead you to a state of inner joy. You think that pleasure comes from your contact with the objects of the world, but there is an inner and finer joy that you have not yet tasted. Meditation is not a difficult task that you must force upon yourself; once you experience that inner joy you will spontaneously want to meditate as much as you now look forward to some outer pleasures.

Nevertheless, it is very helpful to establish a routine to your meditative practice. Just as you eat at certain times of the day, and look forward to eating as those times approach, so too, by developing the habit of meditating at the same time each day your whole being—your body, breath, and mind—will look forward to meditating at that time.

You should find a simple, uncluttered, quiet place where you will not be disturbed. Sit on the floor with a cushion under you or in a firm chair, with your back straight and your eyes closed. Then bring your awareness slowly down through your body, allowing all of the muscles to relax except those that are supporting your head, neck, and back. Take your time and enjoy the process of letting go, of tension in your body. Meditation is the art and science of letting go and this letting go begins with the body and then progresses to thoughts.

Once the body is relaxed and at peace, bring your awareness to your breath. Notice which part of your lungs are being exercised as you breathe. If you are breathing primarily with your chest you will not be able to relax. Let your breathing come primarily though the movement of the diaphragm. Continue to observe your breath without trying to control it. At first the breath may be irregular, but gradually it will become smooth and even, without pauses and jerks. Continue to be aware of the breath.

Meditation is a process of giving your full attention to whatever is chosen. In this case you are choosing to be aware of the breath. Allow yourself to experience your breathing with all its nuances in an open and accepting way, neither judging nor attempting to control or change it. Open yourself so fully that eventually there is no distinction between you and the breathing. In this process many thoughts will arise in your mind: "Am I doing this right? When will this be over? My nostril is clogged— should I get up and blow my nose before I continue? Perhaps I should have closed the window. I forgot to make an important call. My neck hurts." Hundreds of thoughts may come before you and each thought will call forth some further response: a judgement, an action, an interest in pursuing the thought further, an attempt to get rid of the thought. At this point, if you simply remain aware of this process instead of reacting to the thought, you will become aware of how restless your mind is. It tosses and turns like you do on a night when you cannot fall asleep. That is only a problem when you identify with the mind and react to the various thoughts it throws at you. Then, you will be caught in a never-ending whirlwind of restless activity. However if you simply attend to these thoughts when they arise, without reacting, or if you react and attend to the reaction, then they cannot really disturb you. Remember: it is not the thoughts that disturb you but your reaction to them. It is not a sound that disturbs your meditation, but your reaction to it.

Meditation is very simple. It is simply attending. You can begin by attending to your breath, and then if a thought comes, attend to it, notice it, be open to it and it will pass on. Then you can come back to the breath. Your normal response is to react to all your thoughts, and this keeps you ever-busy in a sea of confusion. Meditation is unique in that it teaches you to attend to what is taking place within, without reacting, and this makes all the difference. It brings freedom from the mind and its meandering. In this freedom you begin to experience who you are, distinct from your mental turmoil. You experience inner joy and contentment, you experience relief and inner relaxation, and you find a respite from the tumultuousness of your life—an inner vacation.

However, this inner vacation is not a retreat from the world. It is the foundation of finding inner peace, so that you can apply yourself in the world more effectively. You must also learn to apply the principle of meditation in your worldly activities. Ordinarily, you react to the experiences that come before you in the world in much the same way that you react to your thoughts. If someone says something negative to you, you become upset or depressed. If you lose something you also react emotionally. Your mood depends on what comes before you, and as a result, your life is like a roller coaster ride. Through practicing mediation in your life you can learn to be open to what comes before you in the world, giving it your full attention. Usually, you react before you have fully experienced it; what you see or hear immediately pushes a button. You interpret that according to your expectations, fears, prejudices, or resistances. Thus, you short-circuit the experiences, and you limit yourself to one or two conditioned responses. You give up your ability to respond to a situation openly and creatively. But if you apply the principle of meditation in that situation, you can fully attend to what is occurring. Then, if there is an initial reaction you can also attend to that as well, without reacting to your reaction. "Oh, look at how threatened I feel by that." You need not deny your reaction, let yourself be open to experiencing it and it will move through you and allow other spontaneous responses to also come forward, so that you can select the one that is most helpful in that situation.

In this way meditation is very therapeutic. It not only leads to inner balance and stability, but it also does so by exposing your inner complexes, your immaturities, your unproductive reflexes and habits. Instead of living in these and acting them out, they are brought to your attention, and you can give them your full attention. Then, and only then, will they be cleared.

This method of meditation is an inner method, which has been thoroughly explored for centuries by the great sages. There are various channels for acquiring knowledge—knowledge gained through the mind, knowledge received through the senses, and knowledge obtained through instincts—but the finest of all is intuitive knowledge, which has been the guide of all great men in the past. To reach the infinite library of intuition within is not easy; it is a difficult task, but it is not impossible. Just as a scholar works hard to accomplish his task in any academic field, so also should the meditator collect the teachings from various traditions and examine these methods before he applies a particular method that is suitable to him.

Meditative scholars instruct the student in how to be free from external influences, and how to follow the primary steps, so that the body, senses, and mind are prepared for meditative experiences. If these preliminaries are ignored, then the student may waste years and years in hallucination and fantasy, simply feeding his ego and not attaining any valid or deeper experiences. A valid experience is the deep experience which can guide the student. A human being may have experiences on many levels, but not all experiences guide him. A valid experience is so clear that he does not need any external evidence to support that experience. Such an experience is gained only when the student attains a state of equanimity and tranquility.

In the same way that a student makes a sincere effort to find a competent teacher and a suitable method of meditation, so also does a teacher remain in search of good students who are fully prepared to take this voyage--the voyage from the known to the unknown. Doubts and fears may arise in the mind on various occasions, but when the student decides to tread the path of meditation, he sincerely prepares and disciplines himself. He examines all his "instruments" in the laboratory of life; body, senses, breath, and mind are attuned toward meditation alone.

Those who have been researchers in the external world, who have examined its pleasures and joys, discover that the highest of all joys is meditation, and this joy leads to that eternal joy called *samadhi.* Such great ones like to keep their eyes partially closed, looking into the innermost light that shines within this frame of life.

According to our tradition, which is a meditative tradition more than five thousand years old, mantra and meditation are inseparable, just like two sides of a coin. Some shallow methods that have been taught to students lead one only so far, but the systematic method of meditation can help a student to attain the highest of all states. To practice the method of meditation, one should not dive into shallow waters, for the pearls of life are found in the deep ocean and not in ponds, lakes, or rivers.

During deep meditation, the great sages heard certain sounds called mantras. In the Bible, it is said that those who have an ear to hear will hear. When the mind becomes attuned, it is capable of hearing the voice of the unknown. The sounds that are heard in such a state do not belong to any particular language, religion or tradition.

There are two types of sounds: the sounds that are created by the external world and heard by the ears, and those sounds heard in deep meditation. This sound is called *anahata nada*—the unstruck sound. Inner sounds, which are heard in deep meditation by the sages, do not vibrate in exactly the same way as sound vibrates in the external world. These inner sounds have a leading quality. They lead the meditator towards the center of silence within. The following simile can help in understanding this: imagine that you are standing on the bank of a river and you hear the current as it flows. If you follow the river upstream, you will come to its origin. There, you will find that there is no sound. In the same way, a mantra leads the mind to the silence within. That state is called "soundless sound."

The mantra imparted by a teacher to a student is not at all a commercial proposition. It is like a prescription given to a patient. There are innumerable sounds, each with different effects. The teacher must understand which best suits a particular student, according to his or her attitudes, emotions, desires, and habits.

A mantra has four bodies or *koshas* (sheaths). First, as a word, it has a meaning; another more subtle form is its feeling; still more subtle is a deep intense and constant awareness or presence, and the fourth or most subtle level of the mantra is soundless sound.

Many students continue repeating or muttering their mantra throughout life, but they never attain a state of *ajapa japa*—that state of constant awareness without any effort. Such a student strengthens his awareness, but meditates on the gross level only.

The mantras that are used for meditation in silence are special sets of sounds that do not obstruct and disturb the flow of breath, but help regulate the breath and lead to *sushumna* awakening, in which the breath flows through both nostrils equally. This is a state in which the breath and mind function in complete harmony. The application of sushumna creates a joyous state of mind. When one attains this state, the mind is voluntarily disconnected from the dissipation of the senses. Then, the student has to deal with the thoughts coming forward from the storehouse of merits and demerits—the unconscious mind. The unconscious is a vast reservoir in which we store all the impressions of our lifetime. The conscious mind has the habit of recalling these memories from the deep levels of the unconscious. The mantra helps one to go beyond this process. Mantra creates a new groove in the mind and the mind then begins to spontaneously flow into the groove created by mantra. When the mind becomes concentrated, one-pointed, and inward, it peers into the latent part of the unconscious and there, sooner or later, finds a glittering light.

The most important role that mantra plays is during the transition period that every human being will experience. A dying person wants to communicate with his loved ones. The attachment that we create for mortal things and people produces serious and painful troubles for us at the time of death. Because we lack a clear philosophy, which ought to have been developed during our lifetime, and due to the absence of the practice of meditation and self-experience, our attachments become very painful. Death itself is not painful, but the fear of death is very painful, especially for those who have not pondered the mystery of birth, death, and the hereafter. In such cases, these last moments of life cause extreme discomfort and even affect the voyage after death. This subtle observation leads me to declare that the depth of prayer, contemplation, and meditation should be taught, practiced, and experienced with full honesty, clarity of mind, and one-pointedness.

A dying person's senses do not function properly. He or she gradually loses the sense of sight, the tongue mumbles words that cannot be understood by others, and he or she is unable to express the mind's thoughts in speech or actions. This painful and pitiable situation frightens the mind of a non-meditator. But if one remembers the mantra for a long time in such a state of loneliness, the mantra begins to lead him, and this miserable period of loneliness and agony is over when the mantra becomes his leader. Only one thought pattern is strengthened by remembering the mantra, and it becomes predominant and then leads the individual to his abode of peace, happiness, and bliss. This experience has been validated by me personally after witnessing the death of many sages. I also witnessed the death of many rich men, scientists, and intellectuals, and have observed their experiences of agony. Their facial expressions and helplessness were proof to me that they had not prepared themselves for the last moment of life. I do not recommend any particular mantra from a particular source or tradition, but the power of mantra and meditation can be examined, if you quietly observe a sage, a rich man or an intellectual on his death bed.

To do inner research, mantra and meditation are the

greatest aids to a seeker. Do not disturb your practice of religion, but also learn to know yourself on all levels. Meditation is a concentrated, deep, and intense form of prayer, which is not man-centered prayer, but God-centered prayer.

One who lives in the world can attain the highest state of samadhi through meditation. Then, he is here, yet there; he lives in the world yet above; he includes all and excludes none. When the day arrives that every man, woman, and child practices meditation, we will all attain the next step of civilization and realize the unity in all. Liberation can be attained here and now, and that experience is the ultimate goal of human life.

Glossary

Acharya: a spiritual teacher or instructor. Literally, one whose character and behavior should be followed by others.

Ahamkara: the sense of "I-am-ness." Literally, "the I-maker," or ego. The function of the mind through which pure spirit (purusha) falsely identifies with material and mental creation in the Sankhya and yoga philosophies.

Ahimsa: ahimsa or "non-harming." Ahimsa means non-injuring, non-harming or non-violence. The first of five moral restraints called yamas, which form the first step of the eightfold (astanga) yoga. Their purpose is to curtail behavior which is not conducive to spiritual growth.

Ajapa Japa: that state of constant awareness of one's mantra without any effort.

Anahata Nada: unstruck sound. Inner sounds, which are heard in deep meditation by the sages and lead the meditator towards the center of silence within.

Ananta: limitless.

Antahkarana: the "inner instrument" of the mind, consisting of: manas, or the active mind; buddhi, or the rational and intuitive intelligence; citta, the mind-stuff and the reservoir or subtle impressions (samskaras); and ahamkara, the instrument of identification, the ego, or "I-maker."

Asana: the meditative posture, carefully selected according to the nature and capacity of the student. A good student selects a sitting posture and learns to become accomplished in it.

Bhakti: love plus reverence, to have both reverence and love for the other person.

Bhiksha: the act of begging or asking for alms.

Brahmamurta: three o'clock in the morning, an auspicious time for meditation.

Buddhi: the powerful faculty of intellect. Buddhi is the faculty of mind that has three main functions: it knows, decides, and judges.

Chitta: the pool of subconscious mind-stuff into which all the impressions gathered by the senses are thrown, as it were, and from the bottom of which they rise to create a constant stream of random thoughts and associations.

Devas: "bright beings" or angels.

Dhooni: a kind of fire.

Kama: the first of all the emotions is kama, the prime desire. Kama is the mother of all other desires, and it gives rise to both the desire to satisfy or gratify the senses, and the beneficial desire to help others selflessly.

Kosha: body or sheath.

Krodha: the emotion of anger.

Lobha: greed.

Manas: the faculty which produces data for you from the external world. It is also the function which doubts and questions.

Mantra: a sacred word with a profound meaning usually repeated and contemplated upon by meditators.

Mantra setu: the practice which helps the meditator make the mind one-pointed and inward, and then finally leads to the Center of Consciousness.

Moha: attachment, the sense "This is mine!"

Muda: pride.

Nirodha: control; not in the sense of suppression, but channeling or regulating.

Niyamas: the set of five personal commitments or observances. The second limb of the "eight-limbed" system of Raja Yoga described in the *Yoga Sutras* of Patanjali. The niyamas attempt to cultivate positive habits which are conducive to self-realization.

Prana: the life force. In the yogic tradition, the life force prana is said to be tenfold, depending on its nature and function.

Preyas: there are two categories of objects described in the Upanishads: shreyas and preyas. Preyas means that which is pleasant, and shreyas means that which is helpful.

Rajas: one of the gunas (attributes of prakrti); activity. Rajas impels and energizes, overcoming stagnation.

Samadhi: spiritual absorption; the eighth rung of raja yoga. The tranquil state of mind in which fluctuations of the mind no longer arise.

Samskaras: subtle impressions of past actions.

Sankalpa vikalpa: constant doubt in the mind.

Satsanga: company of the sages.

Sattva: a guna (attribute of prakrti). The sattva guna is characterized by purity, luminosity, lightness, harmony and the production of pleasure. It is the purest aspect of the three gunas.

Seva: the word "service" in Sanskrit is seva, which also means "to enjoy."

Shadi: "happiness" or "marriage."

Shreyas: there are two categories of objects described in the Upanishads: shreyas and preyas. Shreyas means that which is helpful.

Sushumna: the "central channel" through which kundalini energy is said to rise.

Tamas: a guna. The tamas guna is characterized by solidity, stagnation, dullness, inertia, darkness, stasis, stupor.

Upanishad: the final portion of the Vedas; the ancient scriptures containing the wisdom of the sages. The philosophy of Vedanta is based on the Upanishads.

Vairagya: dispassion or non-attachment. According to the Bhagavad Gita, one does not necessarily need to renounce the world or what one needs, but one should perform his duties lovingly, skillfully, and selflessly, remaining unattached to the fruits of his actions.

Yamas: restraints; the first of the eight angas of yoga: non-violence (ahimsa), non-lying (satya), non-stealing (asteya), control of passions, senses, and mind (brahmacharya), and non-attachment (aparigraha).

Index of Sanskrit Terms

ABOUT THE AUTHOR

BORN IN 1925 in northern India, Swami Rama was raised from early childhood by a great Bengali yogi and saint who lived in the foothills of the Himalayas. In his youth he practiced the various disciplines of yoga science and philosophy in the traditional monasteries of the Himalayas and studied with many spiritual adepts, including Mahatma  Gandhi, Sri Aurobindo, and Rabindranath Tagore. He also traveled to Tibet to study with his grandmaster.

He received his higher education at Prayaga, Varanasi, and Oxford University, England. At the age of twenty-four he became Shankaracharya of Karvirpitham in South India, the highest spiritual position in India. During this term he had a tremendous impact on the spiritual customs of that time: he dispensed with useless formalities and rituals, made it possible for all segments of society to worship in the temples, and encouraged the instruction of women in meditation. He renounced the dignity and prestige of this high office in 1952 to return to the Himalayas to intensify his yogic practices.

After completing an intense meditative practice in the cave monasteries, he emerged with the determination to serve humanity, particularly to bring the teachings of the East to the West. With the encouragement of his master, Swami Rama began his task by studying Western philosophy and psychology. He worked as a medical consultant in London and assisted in parapsychological research in Moscow. He then returned to India, where he established an ashram in Rishikesh. He completed his degree in homeopathy at the medical college in Darbhanga in 1960. He came to the United States in 1969, at the direction of his master, bringing his knowledge and wisdom to the West. His teachings combine Eastern spirituality with modern Western therapies.

Swami Rama was a freethinker, guided by his direct experience and inner wisdom, and he encouraged his students to be guided in the same way. He often told them, "I am a messenger, delivering the wisdom of the Himalayan sages of my tradition. My job is to introduce you to the teacher within."

In 1970, upon the invitation of Dr. Elmer Green of the Menninger Foundation of Topeka, Kansas, Swami Rama was a consultant in a research project investigating the voluntary control of involuntary states. He participated in experiments that helped to revolutionize scientific thinking about the relationship between body and mind, amazing scientists by his demonstrating, under laboratory conditions, precise conscious control of autonomic physical responses and mental functioning, feats previously thought to be impossible.

Swami Rama founded the Himalayan International

Institute of Yoga Science and Philosophy, the Himalayan Institute Hospital Trust in India, and many centers throughout the world. He is the author of numerous books on health, meditation, and the yogic scriptures. Swami Rama left his body in November 1996.

The main building of the Institute headquarters, near Honesdale, Pennsylvania.

THE HIMALAYAN INSTITUTE

FOUNDED IN 1971 by Swami Rama, the Himalayan Institute has been dedicated to helping people grow physically, mentally, and spiritually by combining the best knowledge of both the East and the West.

Our international headquarters is located on a beautiful 400-acre campus in the rolling hills of the Pocono Mountains of northeastern Pennsylvania. The atmosphere here is one to foster growth, increased inner awareness, and calm. Our grounds provide a wonderfully peaceful and healthy setting for our seminars and extended programs. Students from around the world join us here to attend programs in such diverse areas as hatha yoga, meditation, stress reduction, Ayurveda, nutrition, Eastern philosophy, psychology, and other subjects. Whether the programs are for weekend meditation retreats, week-long seminars on spirituality, months-long residential programs, or holistic health services, the attempt here is to provide an environment of gentle inner progress. We invite you to join with us in the ongoing process of personal growth and development.

The Institute is a nonprofit organization. Your membership in the Institute helps to support its programs. Please call or write for information on becoming a member.

Institute Programs, Services, and Facilities

Institute programs share an emphasis on conscious holistic living and personal self-development, including:

- Special weekend or extended seminars to teach skills and techniques for increasing your ability to be healthy and enjoy life
- Meditation retreats and advanced meditation and philosophical instruction
- Vegetarian cooking and nutritional training
- Hatha yoga workshops
- Hatha yoga teachers training
- Residential programs for self-development
- Holistic health services, Pancha Karma, and Ayurvedic Rejuvenation Programs through the Institute's Center for Health and Healing.

A *Quarterly Guide to Programs and Other Offerings* is free within the USA. To request a copy, or for further information, call 800-822-4547 or 570-253-5551, fax 570-253-9078, e-mail bqinfo@HimalayanInstitute.org, write the Himalayan Institute, RR 1 Box 1127, Honesdale, PA 18431-9706 USA, or visit our Web site at www.HimalayanInstitute.org.

The Himalayan Institute Press

The Himalayan Institute Press has long been regarded as "The Resource for Holistic Living." We publish dozens of titles, as well as audio and video tapes, that offer practical methods for living harmoniously and achieving inner balance. Our approach addresses the whole person—body, mind, and spirit—integrating the latest scientific knowledge with ancient healing and self-development techniques.

As such, we offer a wide array of titles on physical and psychological health and well-being, spiritual growth through meditation and other yogic practices, as well as translations of yogic scriptures.

Our yoga accessories include the Japa Kit for meditation practice, The Neti™ Pot, the ideal tool for sinus and allergy sufferers, and The Breath Pillow,™ a unique tool for learning health-supportive diaphragmatic breathing. The Varcho Veda™ line of quality herbal extracts is now available to enhance balbanced health and wellbeing.

Subscriptions are available to a bimonthly magazine, *Yoga International,* which offers thought-provoking articles on all aspects of meditation and yoga, including yoga's sister science, Ayurveda.

For a free catalog call 800-822-4547 or 570-253-5551, e-mail hibooks@HimalayanInstitute.org, fax 570-253-6360, write the Himalayan Institute Press, RR1, Box 1129, Honesdale, PA 18431-9709, USA, or visit our Web site at www.HimalayanInstitute.org.